D0006822

GUIDE TO THE STUDY OF
INTERNATIONAL RELATIONS

Chandler Publications in
POLITICAL SCIENCE

VICTOR JONES, *Editor*

Guide to the Study of
International Relations

J. K. Zawodny

UNIVERSITY OF PENNSYLVANIA

CHANDLER PUBLISHING COMPANY

124 Spear Street, San Francisco, California 94105

Copyright © 1966 by Chandler Publishing Company
Library of Congress Card Catalog No. 65–16765
Printed in the United States of America

Certain material included in this book is copyright at the dates listed below, by the authors and publishers named:

Hans Aufricht. *Guide to League of Nations Publications: A Bibliographical Survey of the World of the League, 1920–1947.* New York: Columbia University Press, 1951, pp. xix+682. All material identified in parentheses thus: (Aufricht).

Brenda Brimmer. *A Guide to the Use of United Nations Documents, Including Reference to the Specialized Agencies and Special U.N. Bodies.* Dobbs Ferry, N.Y.: © Copyright 1962 by Oceana Publications, Inc. All rights reserved. Reprinted by permission. Pp. xv+121. All material identified in parentheses thus: (Brimmer).

Everett S. Brown. *Manual of Government Publications: United States and Foreign.* New York: Copyright 1950, Appleton-Century-Crofts, Inc. Reprinted by permission of Appleton-Century-Crofts. Pp. ix+121. All material identified in parentheses thus: (Brown).

Evan Ira Farber. *Classified List of Periodicals for the College Library.* 4th ed. Boston: The F. W. Faxon Company, Inc., 1957, pp. xi+146. All material identified in parentheses thus: (Farber).

Arthur J. Walford, ed. *Guide to Reference Material.* London: The Library Association, 1959, pp. viii+543. *Supplement,* 1963, pp. vii+370. Acknowledgment is made to Dr. A. J. Walford and to the Library Association for permission to reproduce entries from *Guide to Reference Material* and *Supplement.* All material identified in parentheses thus: (Walford).

Fredrica Harriman Whyte. *Whyte's Atlas Guide.* New York: The Scarecrow Press, Inc., 1962, pp. 172. All material identified in parentheses thus: (Whyte).

C. M. Winchell, *Guide to Reference Books.* 7th ed. American Library Association, 1951, pp. xvii+645. 4 *Supplements.* All material identified in parentheses thus: (Winchell).

Z
6461
.Z3

To Charles Fairman

YOUNGSTOWN UNIVERSITY
LIBRARY

153369

Contents

vii

Preface

Contemporary study of International Relations is analytical rather than descriptive. Relying heavily on disciplines other than Political Science, it requires the student to find widely scattered and often complex materials—government documents, national archives, United Nations publications, and up-to-date, empirically validated findings in the behavioral sciences, to name but a few. This volume was designed to aid the student and researcher in finding these diverse materials—to collect between the covers of one book sources which are useful for locating (and, in some instances, understanding) materials in the field of International Relations.

This is an arrangement of *selected* sources. It is not intended to be a catalog of all the material useful or relevant to the study of International Relations. The more than 500 cross-indexed entries which have been classified under subject headings and which, except for the journals, have been annotated, were chosen because they can guide the researcher most efficiently in selecting from several million titles the specific ones he desires.

Department of Political Science   J. K. ZAWODNY
Wharton School, University of Pennsylvania

ix

Acknowledgments

To the initial suggestion (and frequent insistence) of Professor Alvin Z. Rubinstein, my friend and colleague at the University of Pennsylvania, this book, which began as a bibliography for my course in International Relations, owes its existence.

Other persons who have generously contributed and to whom I am deeply grateful include Miss Myrna Stepansky, my research assistant at the Center for Advanced Study in the Behavioral Sciences at Stanford (her diligence and attention to details saved me from many a burden); Mrs. Arline Paul, Head of the Reference Department, the Hoover Institution on War, Revolution and Peace, Stanford, who graciously gave her time and suggestions for arranging the materials; Miss Marjorie Karlson, Head of the Reference Department, Olin Library, Washington University; the staff of the Center for Advanced Study in the Behavioral Sciences; Mrs. Aina Kruger, the staffs of the Humanities, Documents, and Law Libraries at Stanford University; appreciation is expressed to the staff of the British Museum Library in London for their assistance in locating materials and for general helpfulness while I was working there; and, as always, Punia was there.

I have included, with the permission of the publishers and copyright owners, certain material previously published, and here I gratefully acknowledge these permissions. The list of them, in compliance with the requirements of copyright procedure, appears on the verso of the title page.

The imperfections in this book are the author's responsibility.

J. K. Z.

KEY TO THE GUIDES TO LITERATURE CITED

Aufricht

Aufricht, Hans. *Guide to League of Nations Publications: A Bibliographical Survey of the Work of the League, 1920–1947.* New York: Columbia University Press, 1951, pp. xix+682.

Brimmer

Brimmer, Brenda. *A Guide to the Use of United Nations Documents, Including Reference to the Specialized Agencies and Special U.N. Bodies.* Dobbs Ferry, N.Y.: Oceana Publications, 1962, pp. xv+121.

Brown

Brown, Everett S. *Manual of Government Publications: United States and Foreign.* New York: Appleton-Century-Crofts, Inc., 1950, pp. ix+121.

Conover

U.S. Library of Congress, General Reference and Bibliography Division. *A Guide to Bibliographic Tools for Research in Foreign Affairs.* Compiled by Helen F. Conover. 2nd ed. Washington, 1958, pp. iii+145+15-page supplement.

Farber

Farber, Evan Ira. *Classified List of Periodicals for the College Library.* 4th ed. Boston: The F. W. Faxon Company, Inc., 1957, pp. xi+146.

Walford

Walford, Arthur J. *Guide to Reference Material.* London: The Library Association, 1959, pp. viii+543. Supplement, 1963, pp. vii+370.

Whyte

Whyte, Fredrica Harriman. *Whyte's Atlas Guide.* New York: The Scarecrow Press, Inc., 1962, pp. 172.

Winchell

Winchell, C. M. *Guide to Reference Books.* 7th ed. Chicago: American Library Association, 1951, pp. xvii+645. 4 Supplements.

GUIDE TO THE STUDY OF
INTERNATIONAL RELATIONS

HOW TO CITE SOURCES

Scholars and publishing houses have their individual preferences. The following paperbacks are suggested as excellent introductions into a professional and systematic style of citation.

Turabian, Kate L. **A Manual for Writers of Term Papers, Theses, and Dissertations.** Chicago and London: The University of Chicago Press, 1955, pp. vii+110. Now published by Phoenix Books, an imprint of the University of Chicago Press.

A Uniform System of Citation: Forms of Citation and Abbreviations. 10th ed. Cambridge, Mass.: The Harvard Law Review Association, 1964, pp. iv+124. Excellent source for citing judicial, statutory, quasi-statutory, and secondary materials. Also has sections on foreign citations, general rules of citations, and general rules of style.

United Nations, Dag Hammarskjold Library. **Bibliographical Style Manual.** Bibliographical Series No. 8. New York, 1963, pp. vi+62. It specifically suggests how to cite books and pamphlets, periodicals and newspapers, parts of books, government publications, United Nations documents, League of Nations documents, and also suggests appropriate abbreviations.

Abstracts

The contemporary study of International Relations appears to have three characteristics: It is interdisciplinary, analytical, and empirically oriented. In view of this, abstracts which are included will permit the student or researcher to survey the pertinent literature in more than 4,000 academic journals in many languages. The abstracts are, as a rule, well indexed and can be quickly scanned for materials bearing on the subject of International Relations. If the abstract content for the given article (or book) is appropriate, then its citation can be used in locating the original. Of particular importance to the understanding of International Relations is the material appearing in *Psychological Abstracts* and *Sociological Abstracts.*

Abstracts of World Medicine: A Monthly Critical Survey of Periodicals in Modioino and itn Appliod Soionooo. London: Britioh Modioal Association, 1947-. Monthly.

Astronautics Information Abstracts. Pasadena, California: Reports Dept., Jet Propulsion Laboratory, 1959-. Monthly.

Computer Abstracts. London: Technical Information Co., Ltd., 1957-. Monthly. (Supplement: *Computer News*)

Current Thought on Peace and War: A Semi-Annual Digest of Literature and Research in Progress on the Problems of World Order and Conflict. Durham, N.C., 1960-. An abstract journal reviewing materials and research bearing on international security, peace, and the prevention of war. Beginning with the Fall/Winter 1961 issues, abstracts covering research done abroad were presented. These were the first results of a program to expand coverage to at least 70 International Relations centers throughout the world.

Dissertation Abstracts: Abstracts of Dissertations and Monographs in Microform. Ann Arbor, Michigan: University Microfilms, Inc., 1938-. Issued monthly, abstracts are currently given for doctoral dissertations from approximately 140 institutions. Issues contain subject and author indexes, and each year issue No. 12 has cumulated subject and author indexes for issues 1 through 12.

Economic Abstracts: Semimonthly Review of Abstracts on Economics, Finance, Trade and Industry, Management and Labor. The Hague: Nijhoff, 1953-. Prepared by the Library of Economic Information Service of the Netherlands. Each semimonthly issue contains a subject index. Abstracts are in the language in which the article was published. Some are in English; others in French, German, etc. Articles are abstracted from publications in the social sciences, applied sciences, medicine, technology, the arts, architecture, and entertainment. An annual index is published.

Historical Abstracts, 1775–1945: Bibliography of the World's Periodical Literature. Santa Barbara, Calif.: Clio Press, 1955-. A quarterly publication. Arrangement is in sections, the first being a general one covering the entire period, followed by divisions 1775–1815, 1815–1871, etc. These are subdivided into general history and history by country or area. There are in each issue several paragraphs on the scope and methods used in preparation of the abstracts. A five-year index was published in 1963.

International Political Science Abstracts. Oxford: Basil Blackwell, 1951-. Quarterly. "Prepared by the International Political Science Association and the International Studies Conference, with the support of the Coordination Committee on Documentation in the Social Sciences. Each number contains some 350 abstracts . . . each of 100–200 words; about 150 journals are abstracted. In V. 1 the arrangement is systematic, with broad subject group; author and subject index. Thereafter the arrangement has been alphabetical by author, with cumulated subject and author indexes in no. 4 issue of each year. Abstracts of articles in English are given in English; abstracts of articles in any other language are given in French." (Walford, p. 105)

Psychological Abstracts. Lancaster, Pa.: American Psychological Association, 1927-. Originally monthly, now bimonthly. Under eleven major headings, it covers more than 500 (in 1964) learned journals in many languages. The headings most directly useful to the student of International Relations are "General"; "Social Psychology"; "Industrial and Military Psychology." The annual cumulations have authors' index, subject index, list of journals represented in the volume, and a list of abstractors.

Sociological Abstracts. New York: Sociological Abstracts, Inc., 1952-. Published, under the co-sponsorship of the International Sociological Association, the Eastern Sociological Society, and the Midwest Sociological Society, nine times a year. In January 1964 the classification system was revised to prepare for eventual computer storage of information. The abstracts are arranged according to 21 information areas, including social psychology, group interactions, culture and social structure, complex organizations, social change and economic development, mass phenomena, political interactions, social control, demography, etc. Information areas are printed in such a way that they can be supplied individually to subscribers with specialized interests. An index is published periodically for each information area. Abstracts are cross-referenced according to information areas. Abstracts are all in English, though taken from publications throughout the world. Publications used are listed following each information area.

Soviet Periodical Abstracts: Asia, Africa, and Latin America. New York: Slavic Languages Research Institute, 1961-. A quarterly publication. The first title was *Selective Soviet Annotated Bibliographies: Asia, Africa, and Latin America.* Articles on these areas are abstracted from selected Soviet periodicals. Sources of available translations are given.

Soviet Periodical Abstracts: Soviet Society. New York: Slavic Languages Research Institute, 1961-. A quarterly publication, originally titled *Selective Soviet Annotated Bibliographies: Soviet Society.* Articles are abstracted from current Soviet periodical literature on a variety of subjects including public administration and nongovernmental institutions. Sources of available translations are given.

Archives: United States Government

I should like to encourage students in particular to rely heavily on the excellent primary sources in the National Archives. Some items can be purchased from the Exhibits and Publications Division, National Archives, General Services Administration, Washington, D.C. 20402.

U.S. National Archives and Records Service, General Services Administration. **Guide to the Records in the National Archives.** Washington, D.C.: U.S. Government Printing Office, 1948, pp. xvi+684. As of 1964 this is the latest guide listing the records of the National Archives. There are 224 separate compilations of records. For each record group, the National Archives compiles and keeps up-to-date a document entitled "List of Finding Aids" and it also compiles a processed list of "general" finding aids that pertain to more than one record group. For the students of International Relations the most pertinent seem to be the following:

Records of the Office of the Special Adviser to the President on Foreign Trade;
Records of the United States Participation in International Conferences, Commissions, and Expositions;
Records of the Bureau of the Budget;
Records of the Department of State;
Records of the Council of National Defense.

The records in the National Archives may be examined, as a rule, only within the building in which they are housed, except for the fact that agencies of the Federal Government are permitted to borrow records for official use, under some circumstances. Use of some records, particularly those of recent date, is subject to restrictions imposed by Congress. These are listed in Appendix B of the *Guide*. (Introduction, *passim*)

U.S. National Archives and Records Service, General Services Administration. **List of National Archives Microfilm Publications.** Washington, D.C.: U.S. Government Printing Office, 1961, pp. 231.

Describes records reproduced on microfilm, of which positive microfilm copies are for sale. Two hundred sixty microfilm publications listed provide basic documentation for research in political science, as well as economics, law, etc. "For example, nearly 500 rolls of microfilm document diplomatic, consular, and naval relations between the U.S. and . . . China, Japan, and Korea from the late 18th century until 1906." (Introduction, p. v) Table of contents and index to lists should make it possible to locate related materials.

U.S. National Archives and Records Service, General Services Administration. **National Archives Accessions.** Washington, D.C.: U.S. Government Printing Office, 1947-. Annually from 1956. This series begins with No. 31. Nos. 31–50 (July 1947—June 1952) quarterly. No. 51 (June 1954) covered period from July 1, 1952—June 30, 1953. No. 52 (February 1956) covered period from July 1, 1953—June 30, 1955. Nos. 1–30 were supplements to prior volumes of the *Guide to Records in the National Archives.*

U.S. National Archives and Records Service, General Services Administration. **Publications of the National Archives and Records Service.** Washington, D.C.: U.S. Government Printing Office, 1964, pp. 11. This is the most up-to-date and comprehensive listing. It gives titles of: Annual Reports; Bulletins; Staff Information papers; miscellaneous publications; General finding aids (including Guide to the Records in the National Archives, 1948—out of print); Preliminary inventories (159 positions); Reference Information papers; Special Lists; Other finding aids; Record Management Handbooks; Publications of the Office of the Federal Register and the Office of Presidential Libraries (The Franklin D. Roosevelt, The Harry S. Truman Library, The Dwight D. Eisenhower Library, and The Herbert Hoover Library). The listings end with publications of the National Historical Publications Commission.

U.S. National Archives and Records Service, General Services Administration. **Your Government's Records in the National Archives.** Washington, D.C.: U.S. Government Printing Office, 1950, pp. 102. A finding aid.

YOUNGSTOWN UNIVERSITY
LIBRARY

153369

Atlases

Encyclopaedia Britannica. **Encyclopaedia Britannica World Atlas: World Distributions and World Political Geography, Political-Physical Maps, Geographical Summaries, Geographical Comparisons, Glossary of Geographical Terms, Index to Political-Physical Maps.** Chicago: Encyclopaedia Britannica, Inc., 1959. "Geographical Summaries primarily Tables with excellent data not found in any other Atlas, e.g., hydroelectric power; government finance; communication media from TV to number of letters mailed and books published; literacy and education; value of currency in U.S. dollars; as well as products, etc." 78,000 entries; 180 p. maps. (Whyte, p. 22)

Ginsburg, Norton Sydney. **Atlas of Economic Development.** Chicago: University of Chicago Press, 1961, pp. vii+119. (See *Statistics.*)

Hammond's Advanced Reference Atlas: A Collection of Modern and Historical Maps. Maplewood, N.J.: C. S. Hammond & Co., 1956. "This 'complete social studies atlas' in four parts covers
  I. World geography . . .
  II. 'Western Civilization—Historical Maps' . . .
  III. is titled 'Hammond's American History Atlas' . . .
  IV. The world today. This section is frequently up-dated and is very fine." 172 p. maps; about 3,300 entries. (Whyte, pp. 22–23)

A List of Geographical Atlases in the Library of Congress: With Bibliographical Notes (A Continuation of Four Volumes by Philip Lee Phillips). Compiled by Clara Egle LeGear. Washington, D.C.: U.S. Government Printing Office, 1958-. The original 4-volume work published from 1909–1920 was compiled by Philip Lee Phillips. Work has been continued by staff of Library of Congress Map Division. Present 2-volume supplements cover materials to 1955. Vols. 7 and 8 are in preparation. Vol. 5 contains own author list and index. (Preface, Vol. V, p. v)

Rand McNally & Co. **Cosmopolitan World Atlas.** Chicago: Rand McNally & Co., 1959. 159 p. maps; 78,000 entries. "Features of . . . 1955 and 1959 editions include post-war comparison maps, . . .

larger glossary, Tables on Discovery and Exploration. Tables and
Summaries on Climate, economics, political associations." (Whyte,
p. 25)

The Times Atlas of the World. Edited by John Bartholomew. Mid-
century Edition, 5 vols. London: *The Times*, 1955. "With no Gazetteers, no Tables, this collection of Maps is a near perfect, pure
Atlas. The very large scales used permit the inclusion on Maps of
material which in other Atlases appears in Gazetteers, e.g., Highways
from 'Arterial Routes' to 'Tracks'; . . . Air terminals, Pipelines,
Oil Fields, and other locations." 240 p. maps, 220,000 entries.
(Whyte, p. 25)

Whyte, Fredrica Harriman. **Whyte's Atlas Guide.** New York: The
Scarecrow Press, Inc., 1962, pp. 172. *"Whyte's Atlas Guide* is
primarily a subject index to the *Atlases* used in most Public Libraries,
Secondary Schools and Colleges. More than 1,000 entries are classified under 100 Headings." (i.e., Agriculture, Airways and Distances,
Commerce, Discovery and Exploration, Gazetteers, etc. Countries
and continents are also listed under Headings.) (Introduction, p. 17)

Behavioral Sciences: Sources Relevant to International Relations

See also *Abstracts* and *Guides to Literature*.
Two basic guides are recommended (descriptive entries appear in *Guides to Literature*):

Lewis, Peter R. *The Literature of the Social Sciences: An Introductory Survey and Guide.*

White, Carl M., and associates. *Sources of Information in the Social Sciences: A Guide to the Literature.*

Two journals are: *The Journal of Conflict Resolution* and *The American Behavioral Scientist.* (See *Selected Journals Pertinent to International Relations.*)

The following sources are of great value, also:

Berelson, Bernard, and Steiner, Gary A. **Human Behavior: An Inventory of Scientific Findings.** New York and Burlingame: Harcourt, Brace & World, Inc., 1964, pp. xxiii+712. This book presents in the most succinct and incisive fashion contemporary knowledge about human behavior. Chapters on Ethnic Relations, Mass Communication, Opinions, Attitudes and Beliefs, The Society, Culture, and Conclusions are most emphatically recommended to researchers interested in the interdisciplinary approach to the study of International Relations.

Encyclopaedia of the Social Sciences. Editor-in-Chief, E. R. A. Seligman; Associate Editor, Alvin Johnson. 15 vols. New York and London: Macmillan, 1930–1935. (See *Encyclopedias.*)

Essays on the Behavioral Study of Politics. Edited by Austin Ranney. Urbana: University of Illinois Press, 1962, pp. xi+251. Two chapters are of particular interest to the researcher interested in the behavioral approach to international relations. These are entitled: The Impact of the Behavioral Approach on Traditional Political

Science, by Evron M. Kirkpatrick and Some Recent Trends in International Relations Theory and Research, by Richard C. Snyder.

Hinsie, Leland E., and Campbell, Robert J. **Psychiatric Dictionary.** 3rd ed. New York: Oxford University Press, 1960, pp. 788. (See *Dictionaries.*)

Human Behavior and International Politics: Contributions from the Social-Psychological Sciences. Edited by J. David Singer. Chicago: Rand McNally & Co. "Organized in terms of one theoretical approach to comparative foreign policy, the selections in this volume have been included for their empirical, conceptual, or methodological contribution to the discipline of international relations. Included are nearly fifty articles from the postwar literature on sociology and psychology, each preceded by a brief introduction showing the connection with a specific problem." (Rand McNally & Co.) (Forthcoming.)

Human Relations Area Files: Country Survey Series. HRAF Press, New Haven, 1956-. A series of monographs prepared by social scientists from a number of universities by subcontractual arrangement. Each volume deals with cultural life in a particular country or area of the world. Includes, to name a few, Cambodia, Egypt, Iran, Latvia, Poland, Thailand, the USSR, and several African tribes.

The Integration of Political Communities. Edited by Philip F. Jacob and James V. Toscano. Philadelphia and New York: J. B. Lippincott Co., 1964, pp. vii + 314. Empirically validated inquiry into the anatomy of the integrative processes on several levels of human interaction. Includes "Communication Theory and Political Integration" by Karl W. Deutsch; "The Influence of Values in Political Integration" by Philip E. Jacob; and "Models in the Study of Political Integration" by Henry Teune.

International Yearbook of Political Behavior Research. Glencoe, Illinois: Free Press, 1959. (See *Yearbooks: General.*)

Klineberg, Otto. **The Human Dimension in International Relations.** New York: Holt, Rinehart and Winston, 1964, pp. viii+173. An analytical inquiry by a psychologist into the aspects of human behavior with a particular focus on problems of war.

Lasswell, Harold D. **The Future of Political Science.** New York: Atherton Press, 1963, pp. x+256. A distinguished scholar states his concerns about the future of the field and maps out concrete procedures to make it effective in coping with the problems of society. His primary concerns are creativity, basic data survey (storage and retrieval), interaction with other disciplines, and the organizational framework within which the field of political science should operate.

Man and International Relations: Contributions of the Social Sciences to the Study of Conflict and Integration. 2 vols. Edited by J. K. Zawodny. Introduction by Ernest R. Hilgard. San Francisco: Chandler Publishing Company (in preparation). The purpose of this manuscript is to analyze and study violent and nonviolent problem solving on three levels: psychodynamics of the individual, group dynamics, and relations between nation-states. The research covers the period from 1927 to 1964. About 3,200 scholarly journals in disciplines bearing on human behavior, in nine languages, were searched for the materials. Over 200 selections.

Psychological Abstracts. Lancaster, Pa.: American Psychological Association, 1927-. (See *Abstracts.*)

Sociological Abstracts. New York: Sociological Abstracts, Inc., 1952-. (See *Abstracts.*)

Zadrozny, John Thomas. **Dictionary of Social Science.** Washington: Public Affairs Press, 1959, pp. 367. (See *Dictionaries.*)

Bibliographies

Bibliographies of Bibliographies

Besterman, T. A. **A World Bibliography of Bibliographies and of Bibliographical Calendars, Abstracts, Digests, Indexes, and the Like.** 3rd and final ed. 4 vols. Geneva: Societas Bibliographica. 1955–1956. 1st ed. 1939–1940. 2 v. "Alphabetical subject arrangement, with v. 4 as an author index. Records 84,403 separately published bibliographies, excluding general library catalogues but including patent abridgements and list of manuscripts. No annotations except for an estimate, shown in parentheses, of the number of items listed in each work. The major work in its field, including a high proportion of foreign material. The 3rd ed., 'brought down to 1953, inclusive' (Preface), includes material from the bibliographic collections of the Library of Congress. Subject headings used are frequently broad (e.g., Education has 29 sections, one of which, teaching, is further sub-divided into 32 specific subjects). Double entry for composite works is a welcome feature." (Walford, p. 2)

Bibliographic Index: A Cumulative Bibliography of Bibliographies. New York: H. W. Wilson Co., 1938-. "Twice a year, with annual and other cumulations. Covers material published in books, pamphlets, and periodicals since 1937, mostly in English. More than 1,500 periodicals are examined. Arrangement is similar to the other Wilson indexes, but no author index. Particularly useful for minor subjects. Up to and including v. 3, 'complete or comprehensive bibliographies are starred and listed under the subject' (*Directions*, v. 1). This device has since been dropped." (Walford, p. 3)

National Bibliographies

Council of the British National Bibliography, **The British National Bibliography.** London: Whitaker, 1950-. Weekly, quarterly, annual.

"Weekly list has author index, which includes brief entries (giving publisher and price); index to the monthly list cumulates author entries and adds subjects, titles, editors, translators and series. . . . Based on copyright deposit; excludes cheap novelettes, periodicals (except first issues and changed titles), maps, music, and minor government publications. Valuable for its inclusion of non-trade material, society publications, and free items . . . cataloguing is from the books themselves." (Walford, pp. 5–6)

British Union-Catalogue of Periodicals: A Record of the Periodicals of the World, from the Seventeenth Century to the Present Day in British Libraries. Edited by J. D. Stewart, with M. E. Hammond and E. Saenger. 4 vols. London: Butterworth Scientific Publications, 1955–1958. (See *Periodicals: Guides to Periodicals.*)

The Cumulative Book Index: World List of Books in the English Language. New York: H. W. Wilson Co., 1898-. "Frequency varies; now monthly (except August), with frequent paper cumulations, and bound 6-month, annual, 2-year and 5-year volumes. Alphabetical arrangement of authors (with full names), titles, subjects, editors, translators, illustrators, and series; directory of publishers. Since 1928 has attempted to list all books in the English language (with selected pamphlets and government publications), including those published in non-English speaking countries; those appearing in countries other than the U.S., Canada, and Britain are also listed in a separate section by countries (but not in the bound cumulations); gives full bibliographical information, and for books published in more than one country gives all publishers and prices; subject lists of fiction. Not as complete as the individual national bibliographies, but invaluable for books published outside Great Britain; the handiest list because of its frequent cumulation." (Walford, p. 13)

Deutsche Bibliographie. [The German Bibliography.] Bearbeitet von der Deutschen Bibliothek. Frankfurt am Main: Buchhändler-Vereinigung GmbH, 1951-. In progress. Is being compiled by Deutsche Bibliothek (official depository library for West Germany). Includes publications from the four zones of Germany beginning in May 1945, as well as German-language publications from other countries. With a semi-annual index.

The Publishers' Trade List Annual. **Books in Print: An Author-Title Series Index to the Publishers' Trade List Annual.** New York: R. R. Bowker Co., 1948-. The 1964 edition lists approximately 178,000 titles from 1,500 American publishers. The annual volume is divided into two parts—the author index, which usually gives author, title, price, publisher; and the title index, which gives the title, author, price, and publisher. Entries are alphabetical in each index.

The Publishers' Trade List Annual. **Subject Guide to Books in Print: An Index to the Publishers' Trade List Annual.** New York: R. R. Bowker Co., 1957-. This annual volume lists according to Library of Congress headings all of the books appearing in the annual volume of *Books in Print* for the corresponding year. In some cases the same book has been listed under more than one heading by the Library of Congress; consequently, it may appear two or more times in this work. About 133,500 books appear 195,000 times under 28,000 headings and 38,000 cross references. Where books have not been assigned subject headings in the Library of Congress catalog, as for example, with fiction, poetry, and drama, they can best be found in *Books in Print*.

National Libraries Collections

British Museum, Department of Printed Books. **Catalogue of Printed Books.** 95 vols. London: Clowes, 1881–1900. (This catalog was reproduced photographically by the Edwards Co., Ann Arbor, Mich., 1946, in 58 vols.)

————. **Supplement.** 13 vols. London: Clowes, 1900–1905. (This was reproduced in 1950, 10 vols.) The printed catalog of the British Museum Library is primarily an author catalog, giving brief information, usually only author, title, editor, place, and date.

A new edition, revised, added to the original catalog more than 30 years of accessions, gave fuller information, and used more modern cataloging. This edition was titled:

————. **General Catalogue of Printed Books.** 51 vols. (This was published in London and Beccles by Clowes, 1931–1952, Vols. 1–48; in London by Trustees of the British Museum, 1952–1954, Vols. 49–51, when this edition ceased.)

————. **Supplement to Volumes 1–3.** London: Clowes, 1932,

pp. 38. Includes the titles of books added to the Library collections during the printing of these volumes. This edition was followed by:

————. **General Catalogue of Printed Books: Photolithographic Edition to 1955.** London: Trustees of the British Museum, 1959-. This edition is in progress. When completed it is expected that there will be approximately 300 vols. The catalog begins with Vol. 52 and will continue through the alphabet, after which Vols. 1–51 will be done to conform to the rest. When the set is complete, the catalog will contain a record of the books appearing in the collections of the British Museum Library from the 15th century to the end of 1955. (Winchell and supplements, *passim*)

British Museum, Department of Printed Books. **Subject Index of the Modern Works Added to the Library of the British Museum in the Years 1881–1900.** 3 vols. Edited by G. K. Fortescue. London: Trustees of the British Museum, 1902–1903. There are eight 5-year supplements for the period from 1901–1940, published in London, 1906–1944. They are followed by:

————. **Subject Index of Modern Books Acquired 1941–1945.** London, 1953, pp. 1175.

————. **Subject Index of Modern Books Acquired 1946–1950.** London: Trustees of the British Museum, 1961.

The 3 indexes above are arranged alphabetically, and are continued. In the most recent set, the subject headings have been arranged from the *General Catalogue of Printed Books* and photolithographed. (Winchell and supplements, *passim*)

Duignan, Peter. **Guide to African Research Centers and Reference Books.** Stanford, California: The Hoover Institution on War, Revolution, and Peace, Stanford University (in progress).

Hewitt, A. R. **Guide to Resources for Commonwealth Studies in London, Oxford, and Cambridge: with Bibliographical and Other Information.** London: Athlone Press, for Institute of Commonwealth Studies, University of London, 1957, pp. viii+219. (See *Collections and Libraries with Holdings in International Relations.*)

Paris, Bibliothèque Nationale. **Catalogue général des livres imprimés: auteurs.** Paris: Impr. Nat., 1900-. The publication of this catalog is still in progress, 187 vols. having been published as of 1961. Winchell (*Guide to Reference Books*) considers this "An important modern catalog, the value of which . . . cannot be overestimated. . . . The cataloging is excellent. . . ." The arrangement is alphabetical by names of personal authors only (no governments, societies, periodicals, etc.), with title, place and date of publication, publisher, paging, etc., of the original publication being given for reprints. (Winchell and supplements, *passim*)

Ruggles, Melville J., and Swank, Raynard C. **Soviet Libraries and Librarianship: Report on the Visit of the Delegation of U.S. Librarians to the Soviet Union, May–June, 1961, under the U.S.-Soviet Cultural Exchange Agreement.** Chicago: American Library Association, 1962, pp. x+147. This report is "based largely on the notes taken by delegates" while on the mission to the Soviet Union. A bibliography on the subject of Soviet librarianship compiled by Paul Horecky is given in the Appendix.

U.S. Library of Congress. **A Catalog of Books Represented by Library of Congress Printed Cards Issued to July 31, 1942.** 167 vols. Ann Arbor, Michigan: Edwards Bros., 1942–1946.

————. **Supplement: Cards Issued August 1, 1942–December 31, 1947.** 42 vols. 1948.
An author and main-entry catalog of books for which Library of Congress cards have been printed. In 1942 the Association of Research Librarians sponsored the project of reproducing a depository set of L.C. printed cards photographically and issuing it in book form for greater availability. The main catalog includes all cards issued to July 31, 1942. The supplement continues with those issued until December 31, 1947.

————. **The Library of Congress Author Catalog: A Cumulative List of Works Represented by Library of Congress Printed Cards, 1948–1952.** 24 vols. 1953. This 5-year cumulation replaced the monthly and quarterly issues and annual cumulations. Some principles and rules of cataloguing were changed in 1947 and are incorporated in this cumulation. Contains not only main entries, but also essential added entries and cross references.

————. **The National Union Catalog: A Cumulative Author List Representing Library of Congress Printed Cards and Titles Reported by Other American Libraries, 1953–1957.** 28 vols. 1958. The title changed to *National Union Catalog* in 1956. This cumulation contains entries for books, pamphlets, maps, and atlases. Serial titles not catalogued by L.C. printed cards are not included but are listed in *New Serial Titles* (see *Guides to Periodicals*). Beginning in January 1956 the catalog expanded to include titles and holdings reported in other libraries, and the monthly and quarterly issues reflected this addition in their titles. Titles vary slightly on monthly issues. Quarterly and annual cumulations.

————. **The National Union Catalog, 1952–1955; Imprints: An Author List Representing Library of Congress Printed Cards and Titles Reported by Other American Libraries.** 30 vols. 1961. This is a supplement to the regular set, and includes titles previously included, with additional locations as well as newly reported titles, many of which are not on L.C. printed cards. There is some duplication. Cross references are given in many cases.

————. **The National Union Catalog: A Cumulative Author List Representing Library of Congress Printed Cards and Titles Reported by Other American Libraries, 1958–1962.** 50 vols. 1963.

————. **The National Union Catalog: A Cumulative Author List Representing Library of Congress Printed Cards and Titles Reported by Other American Libraries, 1963-.** There continue to be monthly issues, quarterly and annual cumulations, as well as the 5-year cumulations which are listed to date. (Winchell and supplements, *passim*)

U.S. Library of Congress. **Library of Congress Catalog; A Cumulative List of Works Represented by Library of Congress Printed Cards: Books—Subjects, 1950–1954.** 20 vols. Ann Arbor, Michigan: J. W. Edwards, 1955. This is the first 5-year cumulation of the Subject Catalog, which was intended as a complement to the Author Catalog, and as a "cumulative subject bibliography of works currently received and cataloged by the Library of Congress" and libraries participating in the cataloging. Quarterly issues with annual cumulations.

————. **Library of Congress Catalog; Books—Subjects, 1955–1959: A Cumulative List of Works Represented by Library of Congress Printed Cards.** 22 vols. Paterson, N.J.: Pageant, 1960. Second 5-year cumulation. (Winchell and supplements, *passim*)

U.S. Library of Congress. **New Serial Titles: A Union List of Serials Commencing Publication after December 31, 1949.** Washington, D.C., 1953-. (See *Periodicals: Guides to Periodicals.*)

Ward, Robert E., *et al.* **Studying Politics Abroad: Field Research in the**

Developing Areas. Boston and Toronto: Little, Brown and Company, 1964, pp. viii+245. (See *Documents: Guides for the Use of Documents.*)

Subject Bibliographies

Aufricht, Hans. **Guide to League of Nations Publications: A Bibliographical Survey of the Work of the League, 1920–1947.** New York: Columbia University Press, 1951, pp. 682. (See *International Organizations: League of Nations.*)

Basic Russian Publications: An Annotated Bibliography on Russia and the Soviet Union. Edited by Paul L. Horecky. Chicago and London: The University of Chicago Press, 1962, pp. xxvi+313. A selective annotated bibliography sponsored by the Coordinating Committee for Slavic and East European Library Resources, on the political and social sciences and humanities, limited to titles published in Tsarist Russia, the Soviet Union, and in other countries in the Russian language. Useful for teaching, study, and research in Russian history and contemporary affairs of the Soviet Union.

Bibliographie Géographique Internationale. Paris: A. Colin, 1891-. Annual. "Begun as an annual supplement to the journal, *Annales de Géographie,* this valuable publication has been for many years a standard bibliographical guide to international studies in geography. Since 1915 it has been issued as a separate annual volume, under the auspices of the Association de Géographes Francais; since 1945 it is published under international auspices also (Union Géographique Internationale), and with the aid of Unesco and the Centre National de la Recherche Scientifique. The volume covering works of 1953, published in 1955, has 590 pages. The entries, some with brief annotations, are classified by subject and area, with full author index and a Table analytique des matières which indicates main subject divisions. The material catalogued involves all aspects of physical, economic, political and human geography." (Conover, pp. 24–25)

Contemporary China: A Bibliography of Reports on China Published by the United States Joint Publications Research Service. Edited by Richard Sorich. Prepared for the Joint Committee on Contemporary China of the American Council of Learned Societies and the Social

Science Research Council. Reprinted by Readex Microprint Corporation, New York, 1961, pp. 99. A bibliography containing all the reports published on China by the U.S. Joint Publications Research Service from its beginning in 1957 through July 1960. Does not include any of the JPRS reports in Social Science series which began in July 1960. Contains all the reports on China translated by this government agency in three parts, the bibliography, a list of abbreviations for Chinese and non-Chinese serials occurring in Part I, and a subject index to the reports in Part I.

Deutsch, Karl Wolfgang. **An Interdisciplinary Bibliography on Nationalism, 1935–1953.** Cambridge, Mass.: Technology Press of M.I.T., 1956, pp. 165. A selective bibliography divided into fourteen sections, the first two of which deal with general surveys and special works on nationalism. Relevant material from special fields (e.g., economics, geography, political science, religion, sociology, etc.) comprises the next eleven sections. The last section lists books and articles on nationalism by geographic area. The compiler makes it quite clear in his introduction that the section does not represent bibliographies for area studies but rather indicates materials illustrating problems of nationalism in general. New edition forthcoming in 1965.

Foreign Affairs Bibliography: A Selected and Annotated List of Books on International Relations. Published for Council on Foreign Relations, 1933-. Vols. covering 1919–1932, 1932–1942, 1942–1952 published by Harper & Bros., New York and London. Vol. for 1952–1962 published by R. R. Bowker Co., New York. "Covers international affairs in the broadest sense, including recent history, economic, military, social and cultural affairs, and political developments in all countries. Coverage is restricted to books and collections of documents. The volume for 1942–52, containing some 9,000 items in 34 languages, has sections: General international affairs.—The world since 1914.—The world by regions. Brief critical annotations; many cross-references; author and title indexes. Supplemented by *Foreign Affairs* (quarterly), the 'Recent books' section of which provides the basis for *Foreign Affairs Bibliography*. The journal also carries a separate list of source material." (Walford, p. 107)

Goodrich, Leland M., and Hambro, Edvard. **Charter of the United Nations: Commentary and Documents.** 2nd & rev. ed. Boston: World Peace Foundation, 1949, pp. 710. (See *International Organizations: United Nations, Guides to Publications.*)

Grandin, A. **Bibliographie Générale des Sciences Juridiques, Politiques, Économiques et Sociales de 1800 à 1925–1926.** 3 vols. Paris: Recueil Sirey, 1926. Supplements 1–19. "Extensive bibliography of monographic works in the French language in the fields of law, politics, economics and sociology. The first three volumes were retrospective, analyzing publications from 1800 to 1925; subsequent supplements have covered the output of one to two years. The latest, Suppls. 18 and 19, have been annual, covering the work of 1949 and 1950 respectively. The compiler's primary interest is in legal literature, various branches of which take up almost half the text of the average volume, e.g., in Suppl. 19, année 1950, p. 8–94 are concerned with sciences juridiques, p. 95–202 with the other social sciences, and p. 203–281 with subject and author indexes. The second part contains area sections, very full for Belgium and Switzerland and France overseas, less so for non-French-speaking countries, and classified sections on finance, political economy and sociology. Entries are for books, theses, offprints of articles and papers, official documents of international bodies. Full bibliographical detail is given, but no annotations." (Conover, p. 15)

International Association for Research in Income and Wealth. **International Bibliography on Income and Wealth: Annotated Quarterly Report.** London: 1948-. Issued in cooperation with the Statistical Office of the United Nations. "References to books, pamphlets and articles are supplied by correspondents in over 30 countries. Entries are briefly annotated, and classified broadly under General Discussion of Concepts, with subdivisions of Income, Wealth, Social Accounts, etc., and Estimates and Analysis by countries. Each number has an author index." (Conover, p. 16)

International Bibliography of Economics [Bibliographie Internationale de Science Économique]. London: Tavistock Publications; Chicago: Aldine Publishing Co., 1955-. Prepared by the International Committee for Social Sciences Documentation, this bibliography, one of four sections of the *International Bibliography of the Social Sciences,* is designed to be "truly international and to include the most important publications relating to [the] discipline . . ." This work is an annual publication. The remaining three sections are the *International Bibliography of Sociology,* the *International Bibliography of Political Science,* and the *International Bibliography of Social and Cultural Anthropology,* each published in separate volumes. Each volume has topic divisions which include, among others in the

1962 volume, Linear Programming, Empirical and Historical Methods, Mathematical Methods, and Micro-Economic and Macro-Economic Approaches.

International Bibliography of Historical Sciences. Edited for the International Committee of Historical Sciences. Paris: 1926-. "This impressive bibliographical contribution to scholarship since its inception has been under international editorship. The references catalogued . . . are primarily of interest for historical studies. They are classified under a plan detailed on five prefatory pages. . . . About half the major headings are concerned with modern times—general works, religious history, history of intellectual culture, economic and social history, history of law, history of relations between modern states. Entries represent monographic publications and articles selected from over 1500 periodicals. There is a full author index in each volume." (Conover, p. 26)

International Bibliography of Political Science [Bibliographie internationale de Science Politique]. Paris: UNESCO, 1954-. Annual. Prepared, like the *International Bibliography of Economics,* by the International Committee for Social Sciences Documentation under the auspices of the International Political Science Association. International in scope, including the most important publications of the discipline. Vol. I covers the publications for the year 1952. In English and in French. Currently published in London by Tavistock Publications and in Chicago by Aldine Publishing Company.

International Bibliography of Social and Cultural Anthropology [Bibliographie internationale d'Anthropologie Sociale et Culturelle]. London: Tavistock Publications; Chicago: Aldine Publishing Co., 1958-. Like the other 3 sections of the *International Bibliography of the Social Sciences* (see annotation, *International Bibliography of Economics*) this annual publication is designed to be international in scope and to include the most important publications of the discipline. Each volume is divided into sections, which include, among others, General Ethnographic Studies of Peoples and Communities, Social Organization and Relationships, and Problems of Acculturation and Social Change.

The International Committee for Social Sciences Documentation. **A Study of Current Bibliographies of National Official Publications: Short Guide and Inventory.** Jean Meyriat, ed. Paris: UNESCO, 1958, pp. 260. In English and French. This work was prepared at the suggestion of the International Committee for Social Sciences Documentation to serve as a guide to and to analyze bibliographical material available on the official publications of all independent national states, and to suggest possible improvements for such bibliographies. Part I discusses the types of official publications, ways to improve methods of publishing administrative documents, means of facilitating the identification of official publications, and how to improve bibliographical control of official publications. Part II consists of an inventory by country of what is available in this type of bibliography. These are only in French for a number of countries, English for Canada and the United States. There is an index to the countries.

League of Nations. **Catalogue of Publications, 1920–1935.** Geneva: 1935. 5 Supplements, 1936–1945. (See *International Organizations: League of Nations.*)

League of Nations Library. **Brief Guide to the League of Nations Publications.** Revised ed. Geneva: 1930, pp. 32. (See *International Organizations: League of Nations.*)

A London Bibliography of the Social Sciences . . . 11 vols. Compiled by B. M. Headicar and C. Fuller. London: London School of Economics, 1931–1955. "The largest subject bibliography of its kind; arrangement is chronological under subjects or their sub-divisions. The form 'Government publications' is a separate sub-division under each heading or sub-heading. Extensive entries under country, with many sub-divisions; bibliographical details are brief, but the presence of a bibliography is indicated." (Walford, p. 90)
    "V. 10–11 cover additions for the period 1950–55 in all languages and also from 1936–1950 in Russian . . ." (Walford, Supplement, p. 46)

Maichel, Karol. **Guide to Russian Reference Books.** Vol. I: **General Bibliographies and Reference Books.** Edited by J. S. G. Simmons. Stanford, California: The Hoover Institution on War, Revolution, and Peace, Stanford University, 1962, pp. 92. (See *Guides to Literature.*)

Roberts, Henry L., *et al.* **Foreign Affairs Bibliography: A Selected and Annotated List of Books on International Relations, 1952–1962.** New York: R. R. Bowker Co., 1964, pp. xxi+752. Fourth *Foreign Affairs Bibliography* published for the Council on Foreign Relations. First volume covering 1919–1932 prepared by William L. Langer and Hamilton Fish Armstrong; second, 1932–1942, by Robert G. Woolbert; third, 1942–1952, by present editor. "An informal bibliography, based largely on the annotated notes appearing quarterly in *Foreign Affairs* . . . [not] . . . a definitive selection of the world's writing and . . . anyone engaged in extensive research must also have recourse to more specialized bibliographies." (Foreword, p. vii). Arranged in three major sections: General International Relations, The World since 1914, and The World by Regions. Extensive table of contents and cross references. Majority of books are in English and Western European languages. Endeavors to cover the significant books rather than every book published on foreign affairs.

Soviet Foreign Relations and World Communism: A Selected Annotated Bibliography of 7,000 Books in 30 Languages. Compiled and edited by Thomas T. Hammond. Princeton, New Jersey: Princeton University Press, 1965, pp. xxiv+1240. A comprehensive bibliography which includes works on four subjects: "Soviet diplomatic and economic relations with all major countries since 1917; Communist movements throughout the world since 1917; various aspects of Soviet foreign policy and Communist tactics (ideology, front organizations, espionage, international law, etc.); and major internal developments in all Communist countries except the USSR. The bibliography is divided into three main parts: Part I, 'Soviet Foreign Relations by Chronological Periods'; Part II, 'Soviet Foreign Relations and Communism by Regions and Countries'; Part III, 'Special Topics.' " (Introduction, vii–viii)

Union of International Associations. **International Institutions and Inernational Organizations: A Select Bibliography.** Compiled by G. P. Speekaert. Brussels: U.I.A., 1956, pp. 116. (See *International Organizations: Other.*)

United Nations Headquarters Library. **Selected Bibliography of Specialized Agencies Related to the United Nations.** Bibliographical Series No. 1. New York: 1949, pp. 28. (See *International Organizations: United Nations; Guides to Publications.*)

U.S. Library of Congress, Census Library Project. **Statistical Bulletins: An Annotated Bibliography of the General Statistical Bulletins of Major Political Subdivisions of the World.** Prepared by Phyllis G. Carter. Washington, D.C.: 1954, pp. 93. This publication is "a listing by country of official periodical bulletins which keep abreast of current statistics on a variety of subjects, i.e., not those devoted to a single branch, such as labor statistics. The entries are annotated at some length to explain the data covered in each." (Conover, p. 59)

U.S. Library of Congress, Census Library Project. **Statistical Year-**

books: An Annotated Bibliography of the General Statistical Year-books of Major Political Subdivisions of the World. Prepared by Phyllis G. Carter. Washington, D.C.: 1953, pp. 123. This study is "a comprehensive survey, retrospective and current, of statistical yearbooks published by governments throughout the world. Items are annotated to explain in detail the data covered. The arrangement is by continent, with subdivision by country, about two hundred countries being included." (Conover, p. 59)

Biographies

There are in existence between 2,500 and 3,000 various compilations of biographical data in many languages. A bibliographical guide to these sources is in preparation by the Gale Research Company: *Biographical Information: Where to Find It* (entry below).

Included here are two sections, the first containing selected biographies, the second being a listing of personnel currently occupying official positions in government and international organizations.

General and Selected
National Biographies

The Asia Who's Who, 1957. Hong Kong: Pan-Asia Newspaper Alliance, 1957, pp. 712. "Concise, biographical information in English for more than 2,000 prominent Asian men and women from 20 countries and states. Includes domiciled non-Asians, e.g., civil servants, teachers, etc. Chinese, Japanese, Korean and Vietnamese names are given in English and native characters. Appendix, p. 593–712, contains the fullest and most up to date information concerning the leaders of Communist China. In some cases the information is as late as December, 1956." (Walford, p. 417)

Biographical Information: Where to Find It. Detroit: Gale Research Company. (In preparation)

Biography Index: A Cumulative Guide to Biographical Material in Books and Magazines. New York: H. W. Wilson Co., 1949-. Published quarterly, cumulated annually. Vol. I covers the period from

January 1946 to July 1949. Intended for both scholarly and popular reference. Scope is comprehensive. Included are books in the English language, wherever published, material from 1,500 periodicals and, in addition, selected professional journals of law and medicine and obituaries from the *New York Times.* The first section gives the names of biographees, dates, nationality, occupation, and reference to source of information. The second section is an index to occupations and professions. A checklist of composite books analyzed is given.

Current Biography. New York: H. W. Wilson Co., 1940-. Earlier volumes were subtitled *Who's News and Why.* Monthly with annual cumulations. Extensive biographical sketches are frequently updated and are often revised between the monthly publication and inclusion in the annual volume. Information is generally obtained by questionnaire. Annual volumes also list heads of organizations. There is a necrology list. The 1950 and 1960 volumes contain cumulated ten-year indexes. The 1964 volume includes a 1961–1964 index, Classification by Profession.

Hyamson, Albert M. **A Dictionary of Universal Biography of All Ages and of All Peoples.** 2nd ed. New York: E. P. Dutton & Co., 1951, pp. 679. This work is actually a key to reference sources where complete biographies of the persons listed can be found. For each person listed there is a brief note indicating nationality, dates of birth and death (if deceased), and profession.

The International Who's Who. 21st ed. London: Europa Publications, 1957, pp. xvi+1032. "First published in 1935. Contains over 10,000 authoritative biographies. Method of selection: persons of international standing from every country are asked for details of their career and experience, and the press of the countries is constantly scrutinized to get up-to-date information about rising personalities as well as established figures. In many cases information is given for persons from countries where no national *Who's Who* exists. Entries give name, title, dates, nationality, education, profession, career, politics, works (scientific, literary, etc.), address." (Walford, p. 409)

The International Year Book and Statesmen's Who's Who. London: Burke's Peerage, 1953-. (See *Yearbooks: General.*)

The Middle East. London: Europa Publications, 1948-. (See *Yearbooks: General.*)

The Times of India Directory and Year-Book, including Who's Who.

Bombay and London: Bennett, Coleman, 1915-. (See *Yearbooks: National.*)

U.S. Congress. **Official Congressional Directory for the Use of the U.S. Congress.** Washington, D.C., 1809-. (See *Biographies: Personnel in Government,* etc.)

Who's Who: An Annual Biographical Dictionary, with Which Is Incorporated "Men and Women of the Time." London: Black, 1849-. *"Scope.* An authoritative dictionary of contemporary biography, the aim being 'to furnish in as compact a form as possible a series of biographical sketches of eminent living persons of both sexes, in all parts of the civilized world.' The criterion of selection is that of 'personal achievement or prominence, and of a man's or woman's interest to the public at large or to any important section of that public.' *Compilation.* Initially a questionnaire is sent to a person chosen for inclusion and thereafter a proof of the entry is submitted annually to the biographee for revision. Death removes the entry to the appropriate volume of **Who was who . . .** but others disappear from the pages of *Who's who* for a variety of reasons, e.g. proofs not returned, no longer of public interest, etc. As these persons will not appear in *Who was who,* it is therefore necessary for all editions of *Who's who* to be retained for a complete record." (Walford, p. 412)

Who's Who in America: A Biographical Dictionary of Notable Living Men and Women. Chicago: A. N. Marquis Co., 1899-. Revised and reissued biennially. Monthly supplements, December 1939 to 1956; quarterly supplements currently. "An authoritative dictionary of contemporary biography, including 'the best known men and women in all lines of useful and reputable achievement—names much in the public eye, not names locally but generally.' The biographies fall into two groups: (1) those selected because of their special prominence or distinction in certain fields; (2) those included arbitrarily on account of their official position or public standing. Includes not only American citizens but all persons of any nationality likely to be of interest to Americans. Supplemented by: **Who was who in America . . .** 2 v. For all persons deleted because of death. **The Monthly supplement.** December 1939 to 1956. **The Supplement to Who's who.** Quarterly since 1957. **Ten-Year cumulative index,** 1939–1949. 'An Alphabetical Listing of All Sketches Appearing in **The Monthly supplement,** 1939–1949, with a separate alphabetical index for 1950.' **Cumulative Index** for 1951–1955. Not all entries are carried forward, and in these instances a reference is given to the volume in which they last appeared." (Walford, p. 422)

World Biography. 5th ed. Bethpage, New York: Institute for Research in Biography, Inc., 1954, pp. viii+1215. "1st ed. 1940. Covers the 'world's notable living artists, writers, scholars, scientists, physicians, jurists, lawyers, religious leaders, educators, philosophers, musicians, statesmen, business heads and military figures . . . selected without political, ideological or racial preference.' Full detailed entries; states specializations, but does not list works. Claims to be 'the largest and most comprehensive international encyclopaedia of contemporary biography.' " (Walford, p. 410)

Personnel in Government, Diplomatic Corps, and International Organizations

Almanac of Current World Leaders. Los Angeles, Calif.: 1957-. Quarterly. Lists world leaders in the news with brief biographical data for all national states in which leadership has changed since last publication, plus listing by nation of heads of state, cabinet ministers with political affiliations. Also includes a chronological listing of events involving changes in government and other important posts.

American Agencies Interested in International Affairs. Compiled by Ruth Savord and Donald Wasson. New York: Council on Foreign Relations, 1955, pp. vii+289. (See *Institutions in the Field of International Relations.*)

Diplomatist: The Review of the Diplomatic and Consular World. London: Diplomatist Publications Ltd., 1947-. Monthly.

Foreign Service Journal. Washington, D.C.: American Foreign Service Association, 1924-. Monthly.

Pan American Union, General Secretariat, Organization of American States. **Chiefs of State and Cabinet Ministers of the American Republics.** Washington, D.C.: 1964, pp. iii+36. Irregular. Lists names of all chiefs of state and ministers, ambassadors to the U.S., the O.A.S., and the U.N. for all American republics.

Pan American Union, General Secretariat, Organization of American States. **Directory.** Washington, D.C.: irregular, 1948–1960; monthly 1961-. Title varies slightly. The *Directory* lists the names and addresses of the representatives and alternates of each member nation of the O.A.S., the dates of appointment of the representatives and alternates. Includes brief notes on the O.A.S. and its regularly scheduled meetings.

United Nations, Secretariat, Protocol and Liaison Section. **Delegations to the United Nations.** New York: 1946-. Gives the membership of the General Committee of the General Assembly, Main Committees and Delegations to the General Assembly by country. Before March/April 1952 issued as *Delegations to the United Nations.* 1952–August 1954 issued as *Permanent Missions and Delegations to the United Nations.* Published each session of the General Assembly.

United Nations, Secretariat, Protocol and Liaison Section. **Permanent Missions to the United Nations.** New York: 1946–1955. It cites, by country, the members of the missions, the addresses and telephone numbers of the missions, and also the national holiday. It lists also membership of Councils and Commissions, and includes a section on "Nonmember states with permanent observers' offices at Headquarters." Before March/April 1952 issued as *Delegations to the United Nations.* 1952–August 1954 the title was *Permanent Missions and Delegations to the United Nations.* Since 1956 this material has been included in *Delegations to the United Nations.* (See above.)

U.S. Congress. **Biographical Directory of the American Congress, 1774–1961: The Continental Congress September 5, 1774, to October 21, 1788, and the Congress of the United States from the First to the Eighty-Sixth Congress March 4, 1789, to January 3, 1961, Inclusive.** Rev. ed. Washington, D.C.: U.S. Government Printing Office, 1961, pp. 1863. Biographical sketches of Senators and Representatives, 1774-. This volume supersedes ten previously published biographical Directories and Dictionaries published between 1859 and 1949.

U.S. Congress. **Official Congressional Directory for the Use of the U.S. Congress.** Washington, D.C.: 1809-. This volume contains a great deal of information about personnel in government, members of Congress, etc., that is particularly useful for members of Congress. There are approximately 21 sections giving the following types of information about members of Congress: the name, district, home address, Washington residence, and biography of both Senators and members of the House of Representatives; lists of the members of Congress by the year in which their terms expire; a list of Senators and Representatives chronologically in terms of the length of their service; the composition of all Congressional committees, joint committees, commissions, and boards; lists of Senators, their administrative assistants and secretaries; lists of Representatives and their secretaries; and statistical information concerning all sessions of Congress starting with the first. There is a description of the Capitol and grounds and several pages of plans of the Capitol Building. Another section is devoted to the Executive branch of government, including the President, members of his Cabinet, the Executive Office of the President, the listing of personnel for each department in the Cabinet, including their names and addresses and a list of independent agencies and their personnel. A similar section is devoted to the Judiciary, giving biographies of current and retired Justices of the Supreme Court, as well as lists of justices for other U.S. Courts, such as the Courts of Appeals and the Courts of Customs and Claims. Another section is devoted to the District of Columbia and its government. Further sections contain lists of international organizations; foreign diplomatic representatives and foreign consular offices in the United States; a list of members of the press galleries; a list of members of the White House News Photographers Association; a section on the periodical press galleries; maps of Congressional districts; and an individual index for members of Congress.

U.S. Department of State. **The Biographic Register.** Prepared by the Division of Publishing Services, Office of Operations. Washington, D.C.: U.S. Government Printing Office, 1869-. Annual. Provides background information on personnel of the Department of State and the Foreign Service, and of other federal agencies participating in the field of foreign affairs.

U.S. Department of State. **Diplomatic List.** Washington, D.C.: U.S. Government Printing Office, 1894-. Quarterly. A listing of the staffs of the diplomatic corps and foreign legations by country. Also includes a list of the order of precedence, and dates of presentation of credentials of ambassadors and ministers from each country.

U.S. Department of State. **Foreign Service List.** Compiled by the Publishing and Reproduction Services Division, Office of Operations. Washington, D.C.: U.S. Government Printing Office, 1857-. Quarterly. Provides information on the assignments of foreign service and other U.S. personnel assigned overseas. Also includes information on the opening and closing of posts, posts changed in rank and status, and similar data. May not reflect current diplomatic status since only includes information received before revision date for publication. Current information on any officer assigned to any overseas post can be obtained by writing to the Department of State, Washington, D.C. 20520.

Who's Who in the United Nations. 1st ed. Yonkers-on-Hudson, N.Y.: C. E. Burckel & Associates, 1951, pp. 580. "No new edition has appeared of this biographical directory, data for which were gathered in the fall of 1950. Consequently many of the 1700-odd sketches of the significant personalities in the international organization are out of date. The coverage was purported to be of representatives, alternates and members of delegations to the Fifth General Assembly, permanent representatives, ranking members of the Secretariat from Chiefs of Sections upward, delegates to specialized agencies. Many of the biographical notes are accompanied by photographs." (Conover, pp. 65–66)

Book Reviews

Please notice that, in addition to the sources cited below, most journals listed in the section, *Periodicals: Selected Journals Pertinent to International Relations,* include a section on reviews of current books, as does *The American Political Science Review.*

The Annals of the American Academy of Political and Social Science. Philadelphia: 1890-.

Book Review Digest. New York: H. W. Wilson Co., 1905-. Monthly issues are cumulated annually into permanent volumes. Lists, according to subject, title, and author indexes, books reviewed in approximately seventy periodicals, both scholarly and popular. To be listed a nonfiction work must have two or more reviews in these periodicals. Generally no more than three reviews are summarized.

An Index to Book Reviews in the Humanities. Detroit: P. Thomson, 1960-. Quarterly until 1963. Now yearly. Through the December 9, 1962 issue, the index was published quarterly and included only reviews written in the English language. As of 1963, the first annual volume, all applicable reviews, regardless of the language, have been indexed. Interpretation of the "humanities" has undergone considerable changes from one volume to the next. Subjects once covered but now excluded are archaeology, theology, and sports; and the social sciences have been de-emphasized.

The New York Times Book Review. New York: 1896-. Title varies. Oct. 10, 1896—June 20, 1920: *The New York Times Review of Books, Literary Section of the New York Times;* June 27, 1920— Dec., 1922: *The New York Times Book Review and Magazine;* Jan. 1923-: *The New York Times Book Review.* (See *The New York Times Index,* "Book Reviews" for exact citation to date, page, and column.)

Politische Literatur: Berichte über das Internationale Schrifttum zur Politik. Frankfurt am Main: Bollwerk-Verlag, 1952–1954. Edited by Institut für Politische Wissenschaft der Johann Wolfgang Goethe Universität. "Journal of reviews of international political science literature. The reviews, signed by scholarly contributors, are of several hundred words each; they analyze critically between 350 and 400 books annually, the selection being from notable writings in English, French, German and other languages. A separate leaflet included with the first number of the following year contains author and subject indexes." (Conover, pp. 19–20) Superseded by *Neue Politische Literatur: Berichte über Das Internationale Schrifttum* (Stuttgart: 1956-).

The Times (London) **Literary Supplement.** London: 1902-. Weekly. "The long critical reviews and short book notes in the weekly literary supplement of *The Times* cover extensively new books in all fields. An annual index of authors and titles provides a handy key for locating evaluative descriptions of almost all books published in England." (Conover, pp. 26–27)

The United States Quarterly Book Review. Prepared by the Library of Congress, 1945–1956. Publisher has varied. New Brunswick, N.J.: Rutgers University Press, March 1945–June 1954; Denver, Colorado: Swallow Press, September 1954–June 1956. Ceased publication June 1956. Published as **The United States Quarterly Book List,** 1945–March 1950. "Review journal containing evaluative descriptions of a selected list of new American books, chosen according to certain specifications as contributions to American thought. The entries are classified according to disciplines, including a category of Social Sciences, which includes economics, political science and other branches of the social studies. The *Quarterly Book Review* is edited with special consideration of the needs of libraries and scholars abroad. The unsigned reviews are contributed by specialists from many universities and other institutions. Probably not more than fifteen or twenty titles per number are of specific interest for studies of current international affairs." (Conover, p. 27)

Collections and Libraries with Holdings in International Relations

British Library of Political and Economic Science, London School of Economics and Political Science, University of London. **Guide to the Collections.** London: British Library of Political and Economic Science, 1948, pp. 136. "The library is probably the largest of its kind in the world, having some 300,000 bound volumes at the time this *Guide* was produced. 16 of the 18 chapters deal with types of material (e.g., general reference books; government publications) and subject material (e.g., statistics, law). Ch. 16 deals with Russian publications. Major and typical items are cited, with annotations. . . . Also includes an index of subjects and collections. A new and revised edition of 'A Reader's Guide.' " (Walford, p. 89)

Conference on Asian Affairs, New York. **American Institutions and Organizations Interested in Asia: A Reference Directory.** Edited by Ward Morehouse. New York: Taplinger Publishing Co., 1957, pp. 510. "A directory of more than 600 universities, religious and educational organizations, foundations, museums and libraries, scientific and professional societies, and other groups, with description of their activities and publications relating to Asia. The programs include teaching and research, technical assistance, student activities, medical and educational missionary work, collections of Asian art and research materials. Appendices are a list of Asian diplomatic and consular offices and services in the United States, and a subject index." (Conover, Suppl., p. 5)

Directory of Special Libraries and Information Centers. 1st ed. Edited by Anthony T. Kruzas. Detroit: The Gale Research Company, 1963, pp. 767. More than 10,000 special libraries and information centers are listed alphabetically by name of sponsoring organization, with information given as to principal subject interest, address, subjects, special collections, holdings, services, publications, staff (partial listing if organization is large). There is a subject index. The book is the first of a planned continuing series.

35

Hewitt, A. R. **Guide to Resources for Commonwealth Studies in London, Oxford, and Cambridge: with Bibliographical and Other Information.** London: Athlone Press, for Institute of Commonwealth Studies, University of London, 1957, pp. viii+219. "Includes a concise survey of library resources by subjects, bibliographies and works of reference and notes on individual collections." (Walford, p. 446)

International Committee for Social Sciences Documentation. **International Repertory of Social Science Documentation Centres.** Prepared for the Dept. of Social Sciences, UNESCO. Paris: UNESCO, 1952, pp. 42. "Issued by the Committee under an earlier name, Coordinating Committee on Documentation in the Social Sciences. This Committee . . . is an autonomous body, which acts as advisor to the Unesco Dept. of Social Sciences, its membership being made up of experts representing various countries and disciplines. Its International Repertory results from a questionnaire circulated to member countries, and offers concise and precise data about leading research institutions in each country. For each institution data are given on direction, organization, subjects covered, publications, and services, the latter including statistics of libraries, card files, etc., as well as special services." (Conover, p. 43)

International Library Directory: A World Directory of Libraries. 1st ed. London: The A. P. Wales Organization, Publishing Division, 1963, pp. 1083. Written in English, French, German, Italian, and Spanish. Type of library and its character is indicated in most cases. Forty main subjects are included in the libraries listed. A code indicates language of collection. Books and periodical collections are indicated.

International Scientific Organizations: A Guide to Their Library, Documentation, and Information Services. Prepared under the Direction of Kathrine O. Murra. Washington, D.C.: Library of Congress, 1962, pp. xi+794. (See *International Organizations: Other.*)

London Library. **Subject Index of the London Library.** London: London Library, 1908. With Supplements. "Valued for its specific headings, adequate cross-references and analytical entries. No personal name entries . . . but a sub-heading 'Biography' appears under many subjects. Under the heading 'Academies' are listed the London Library's holdings of publications of academies and societies. . . . a valuable bibliographical tool, including a fair proportion of foreign material." (Walford, p. 17)

Subject Collections: A Guide to Special Book Collections and Subject Emphases as Reported by University, College, Public, and Special Libraries in the United States and Canada. 2nd ed. rev. & enl. Compiled by Lee Ash. New York: R. R. Bowker Co., 1961, pp. ix+651. This edition contains about 20,000 separate entries and 800 new subject headings have been listed since the first edition. Under the subject heading, International Relations (cross referenced with Diplomacy, Geopolitics, International Cooperation, International Law, International Organization, Munitions, Peace, World Politics) are listed by name institutions of learning, libraries, research organizations, etc., with holdings in International Relations, number of volumes or microfilm reels in the holding, restrictions, if any, on access to the materials. The author indicates that the listings are not complete for the reason that libraries do not generally evaluate their holdings according to any consistent pattern.

United Nations Library, Geneva. **Monthly List of Books Catalogued in the Library of the United Nations.** Geneva: League of Nations, 1928–1945; United Nations, 1946-. " 'A selected list of works relating to questions of every kind studied by the organs of the United Nations.' Carries about 350 items monthly: systematic arrangement in seven groups, on much the same pattern as the *Monthly List of Selected Articles* . . . except that in this case section 7 is devoted to works of reference. U.D.C. classification numbers are given; no annotations." (Walford, p. 90)

United Nations Library, New York. **New Publications in the United Nations Headquarters Library.** New York: United Nations, 1949-. " 'A monthly list of recent books, periodicals and newspapers added to the . . . Library. It is planned as a practical finding list rather than as a bibliography or a list of suggested readings' (Foreword). Publications of the United Nations and specialized agencies are not included." (Walford, p. 90)

U.S. Library of Congress. **The National Union Catalog of Manuscript Collections.** Ann Arbor, Michigan: J. W. Edwards, Inc., 1962-. Planned as a continuing series. Vol. 3 is an index for 1959–1962. Publisher varies. Shoe String Press, Hamden, Connecticut, published Vols. 2 and 3. These three volumes represent the beginning of an attempt to list bibliographically the manuscript resources of American repositories. About 12,000 manuscript collections from 398 repositories have so far been described and indexed.

Dictionaries

Black, Henry C. **Black's Law Dictionary: Definitions of the Terms and Phrases of American and English Jurisprudence, Ancient and Modern.** 4th ed. St. Paul, Minn.: West Publishing Co., 1951, pp. 1882. The first edition was published in 1891. A compilation of terms and definitions used in the practice of law.

Dictionnaire de la Terminologie du Droit International. Publié sous le patronage de l'Union Académique Internationale. Paris: Sirey, 1960, pp. xv+755. This is a dictionary of international law terms used in diplomatic correspondence, treaties, etc.

Haensch, Günther. **Internationale Terminologie: Diplomatie, Verträge, Internationale Organisationen, Konferenzen . . .** Stuttgart: Müller, 1954, pp. 180. A compilation of terms used in diplomacy and international conferences. In German, English, French, and Spanish.

Hinsie, Leland E., and Campbell, Robert J. **Psychiatric Dictionary.** 3rd ed. New York: Oxford University Press, 1960, pp. 788. This edition has been completely revised by R. J. Campbell and many of the definitions have been rewritten in the light of recent developments. "The first edition and supplement contained over eight thousand listings; approximately thirteen hundred of these have been eliminated and nearly two thousand new listings have been added." (Preface, pp. vii–viii)

White, Wilbur W. **White's Political Dictionary.** New York: World Publishing Co., 1947, pp. 378. The dictionary's primary objective is to interpret the political world to the general reader. Only those terms of political content or interest, gleaned largely from the vocabularies of political parties, international relations, and the mechanics of the governing process, are included. Meanings given are those most generally in current use; where any disagreement or ambiguity exists, it has been clearly indicated.

Zadrozny, John Thomas. **Dictionary of Social Science.** Washington: Public Affairs Press, 1959, pp. 367. A compilation of specialized terms from all of the social sciences. "Intended for students, laymen and specialists who desire to become acquainted with the basic concepts of the social sciences without resort to voluminous professional literature." (Preface)

Dissertation Lists

Dissertation Abstracts: Abstracts of Dissertations and Monographs in Microfilm. Ann Arbor, Michigan: University Microfilms Inc., 1938-. Monthly. Published as *Microfilm Abstracts,* 1938–1951. (See *Abstracts.*)

Doctoral Dissertations Accepted by American Universities. Compiled for the Association of Research Libraries. New York: H. W. Wilson Co., 1934-. The first complete annual listing of dissertations, including those unpublished, in the United States, although those in the field of science had been listed annually since 1898, with breaks of several years between 1917 and 1925. Listing arrangement is divided in seven fields, with subfields thereunder. For example, Social Sciences: Anthropology, Economics, Education, etc. Within each subfield the dissertations are listed by university, under the author's name.

"Doctoral Dissertations in Political Science In Universities of the United States and Canada," *The American Political Science Review* (September issue, 1911-). The *Review* begins November, 1906. Dissertations begin 1911. Appears annually in the September issue. Lists and amends the titles of dissertations in progress and completed.

List of Doctoral Dissertations in History Now in Progress at Universities in the United States. Washington: American Historical Association, 1947-. Publishers have varied. First published 1909 by Carnegie Institute. "Arranged under countries and other broad subjects, with author and university indexes." Irregular. No lists for 1942–1946. (Walford, p. 433)

"List of Doctoral Dissertations in Political Economy in Progress in American Universities and Colleges," *American Economic Review* (September issue, 1940-). Doctoral dissertations are arranged by subject. Appears annually in the September issue.

U.S. Library of Congress, Catalog Division. **List of American Doctoral Dissertations Printed 1912–1938.** 26 vols. Washington, D.C.: U.S. Government Printing Office, 1913–1940. Planned to include "every thesis printed, whether separately or in another publication," these to be acquired, classified, catalogued by the Library of Congress and from the catalogue cards an annual list was to be prepared of the dissertations printed in each calendar year beginning 1912. Section I gives a list of theses printed (alphabetical by name of author); Section II gives classified lists, by broad classes, according to the Library of Congress scheme; Section III gives an index of subjects; Section IV gives the list of doctors whose theses have been printed during the year, alphabetically by college or university. The last volume printed contains a supplementary list of theses printed prior to 1938.

Documents

Collections of Documents

A Catalog of Files and Microfilms of the German Foreign Ministry Archives 1920–1945. 2 vols. Compiled and edited by George O. Kent. Stanford, California: The Hoover Institution on War, Revolution, and Peace, Stanford University, 1962. (See *Films: Guides.*)

Communist China 1955–1959: Policy Documents with Analysis. With a Foreword by Robert R. Bowie and John K. Fairbank. Prepared at Harvard University under the Joint Auspices of the Center for International Affairs and the East Asian Research Center. Cambridge, Mass.: Harvard University Press, 1962, pp. xii+611. Includes 48 documents. Its purpose is to present a "documentary introduction to the internal history of Communist China," for the dates given. It is intended as a work of digestion for the general student. Full texts of the documents have been given, with the sources clearly identified. There is a commentary for each chapter, and references to other source material are given for further reading. (Introduction)

Council on Foreign Relations. **Documents on American Foreign Relations.** New York and Evanston, Ill.: Harper and Row, 1952-. Annual. A series of documentary volumes initiated in 1939 by the World Peace Foundation, Boston, and carried on by the Council on Foreign Relations since 1952. The purpose of the series is to make available in a convenient reference form the most important documentary materials concerning foreign relations of the U.S.

General Sikorski Historical Institute. **Documents on Polish-Soviet Relations, 1939–1945.** London: Heinemann, 1961-. In Vol. I (1939–1943, pp. 625) are English translations of the documents, telegrams, conferences, official letters, etc., pertinent to Polish-Soviet relations in the given period. Includes several treaties between the two countries. The materials were gathered, whenever possible, from the original files of the Polish Government-in-Exile and its Executive

Branches including the Chancery of the President of Poland. Arrangement is chronological. Some selected documents 1918- are included. Very well indexed (see pp. xxi–xl).

Great Britain, Foreign Office. **British and Foreign State Papers.** London: H.M. Stationery Office, 1841-. (See *Treaty Collections.*)

Great Britain, Foreign Office. **Documents on British Foreign Policy, 1919–1939.** 3 series. Edited by E. L. Woodward and Rohan Butler. London: H.M. Stationery Office, 1946–1955. First Series, 13 volumes; Second Series, 8 volumes; Third Series, 10 volumes. The First Series begins in 1919 and includes events from the signature of the treaty of peace with Germany, ending World War I, to the year 1930, ending with the two sessions of The Hague Conference. The series was published as a result of the government decision to publish the most important documents in the Foreign Office archives relating to British foreign policy between the years 1919 and 1939. The Second Series begins in March, 1930, and ends on March 8, 1938, the day before the plebiscite was held in Austria. The Third Series was published in order to speed the appearance of documents relevant to the origins of World War II, and it covers the period from March 8, 1938, to September 3, 1939. Volume X is an index.

Great Britain. **Government Publications in Microprint available from Readex Microprint Corporation,** 115 University Place, New York 3, N.Y.: (1) **Hansard.** Parliamentary Debates, House of Lords and House of Commons from year 1066–1918. (2) **House of Commons Sessional Papers 1731–1900.** (3) **House of Commons Sessional Papers Indexes 1696–1900.**

NSDAP Hauptarchiv: Guide to the Hoover Institution Microfilm Collection. Compiled by Grete Heinz and Agnes F. Peterson. Stanford, California: The Hoover Institution on War, Revolution, and Peace, Stanford University, 1964, pp. 175. (See *Films: Guides.*)

Peaslee, Amos Jenkins. **Constitutions of Nations: The First Compilation in the English Language of the Texts of the Constitutions of the Various Nations of the World, Together with Summaries, Annotations, Bibliographies, and Comparative Tables.** 2nd ed., 3 vols. The Hague: Nijhoff, 1956. The first edition of this work was published in 1950 and was the most comprehensive and up-to-date collection of its kind. This work gives the texts of all the constitutions of all the nations of the world with the status of sovereign nations, up to the time of publication, with a summary and bibliographical notes for each country's constitution. Tables at the end of Vol. III give comparisons of all the nations for (1) International Status; (2) Form of Government; (3) Source of Sovereign Power; (4) Rights of the People; (5) Legislative Department; (6) Executive Department; (7) Judicial Department; (8) Area and Population. Vol. III includes an index to all 3 volumes.

Peaslee, Amos Jenkins. **International Governmental Organizations: Constitutional Documents.** 2 vols., 2nd ed. revised. The Hague: Nijhoff, 1961. (See *International Organizations: Other.*)

Royal Institute of International Affairs. **Documents on International Affairs, 1928-.** Edited by J. W. Wheeler-Bennett *et al.* London: Oxford University Press, for the Royal Institute of International Affairs, 1929-. "Intended to accompany and supplement the *Survey of International Affairs,* . . . although it can now be used independently, thanks to the notes prefacing each section. A collection of the available state papers, exchanges of notes, statements, speeches and other source material of a wide range of countries." (Walford, p. 109)

Soviet Documents on Foreign Policy. Edited by Jane Tabrisky Degras. 3 vols. London and New York: Oxford University Press, 1951–1953. Issued under the auspices of the Royal Institute of International Affairs. Volume I covers the years 1917–1924; Volume II covers the years 1925–1932; Vol. III covers the years 1933–1941.

United Nations Documents, 1941–1945. London and New York: Royal Institute of International Affairs, 1946, pp. 271. (See *International Organizations: United Nations Selected Documents and Records.*)

U.S. Department of State. **American Foreign Policy: Current Documents.** Washington, D.C.: U.S. Government Printing Office, 1956-. It is "an annual, one-volume collection of the principal messages, addresses, statements, reports, diplomatic notes, and treaties made in a given calendar year which indicate the scope, goals, and implementation of the foreign policy of the United States" (Preface, p. iii). It continues two earlier publications: *A Decade of American Foreign Policy: Basic Documents, 1941–1949* and *American Foreign Policy, 1950–1955: Basic Documents.* Has a complete list of the documents (printed as a table of contents) and an index. The documents are usually arranged under topical headings within each of the 13 parts.

U.S. Department of State. **The Department of State Bulletin.** Washington, D.C.: U.S. Government Printing Office, 1939-. "Issued by the Public Services Division of the State Department, it provides 'information on developments in the field of foreign relations and on the work of the Department of State and the Foreign Service.' Includes selected press releases on foreign policy, statements and addresses by the President and members of the Department as well as special articles on various phases of international affairs and the functions of the Department. Information is included concerning treaties and international agreements to which the U.S. is or may become a party and other treaties of general international interest. There is also information on international organizations of which the U.S. is a member, especially the United Nations. 'Publications of the Department, as well as legislative material in the field of international relations, are listed currently.' " (Farber, p. 106)

U.S. Department of State. **Documents on German Foreign Policy, 1918–1945: from the Archives of the German Foreign Ministry.** Washington, D.C.: U.S. Government Printing Office, 1949-. Edited by J. R. Sontag and others under the sponsorship of the U.S. Department of State, the British Foreign Office, later joined by the French Foreign Ministry, from captured documents from the archives of the German Foreign Ministry and Reich Chancellery, selected "on the basis of highest scholarly objectivity." A German edition, *Akten zur Deutschen Auswärtigen Politik* (Baden-Baden), and an unofficial French edition, *Les Archives Secrètes de la Wilhelmstrasse* (Paris), have also been published. The *Documents* is issued in two series—Series C, which is to cover the years 1933 to 1937, in six volumes, has four volumes completed, and Series D, for the years 1937 to 1945, has 12 volumes of a projected 13 completed. Volume XII of Series D, published in 1962, ends in June 1941, with the German attack on the Soviet Union.

U.S. Department of State. **Foreign Relations of the United States: Diplomatic Papers.** Washington, D.C.: U.S. Government Printing Office, 1862-. The volumes have had their present title since 1947. The first title of this series was *Papers Relating to Foreign Affairs Accompanying the Annual Message of the President.* The title was changed in 1870 to *Papers Relating to the Foreign Relations of the United States.* These volumes have been compiled on an annual basis by the State Department since the publication of diplomatic correspondence accompanying President Lincoln's first annual message to Congress, December 3, 1861.

The volumes are not current, the Papers and Message for 1943 having been published in 1963. Publication has been continuous since the beginning, except for the year 1869, but there have been more than one volume published per year and there have been supplements, such as the World War Supplements, the 1918–1919 Russia volumes, the Japan supplement 1931–1941, etc. Each volume published during a year is devoted to a specific subject, except for Vol. 1 which contains general papers.

These papers constitute the official record of the foreign policy of the United States, and include all the documentation, subject to necessary security regulations, "needed to give a comprehensive record of major foreign policy decisions within the range of the Department of State's responsibilities . . . with appropriate materials concerning the facts which contributed to the formulation of the policies." (Department of State Regulation 1350, June 15, 1961) The basic documentary record is edited by the Historical Department, Bureau of Public Affairs, Department of State. Each volume has an alphabetical index and table of contents.

These same volumes are also bound in the *Congressional Serial Set* under House Executive Documents or House Documents but are currently listed in *Document Catalogs* only under Department of State publications.

Prior to 1862, the collection of papers and documents relevant to the President's Annual Message to Congress was printed, usually, as House or Senate Documents and can be located in the *Document Catalog* for the year in question, under one of those headings, for many of the years between 1789 and 1861. There are also two collections of State papers which were compiled under the authority of Congress and which cover a part of the period between 1789 and 1861. The first of these is:

American State Papers: Documents, Legislative and Executive, of the Congress of the United States. 38 vols. Washington, D.C.: Gale & Seaton, 1832–1861. The first six volumes cover documents pertaining to Foreign Relations from April 30, 1789—May 24, 1828. The most important legislative and executive documents of the United States, selected by the Secretary of the Senate and the Clerk of the House of Representatives, covering a period beginning 1789 and ending between 1823 and 1838, are contained in these volumes. The volumes on Foreign Relations go only to 1828. The subjects contained in these volumes were divided into ten classes and Class 1 is referred to as Foreign Relations. The documents are in chronological order. Vol. 1 contains speeches and messages of the Presidents from the first administration to 1814.

A second important collection is:

U.S. Congress. **State Papers and Public Documents of the United States from the Accession of George Washington to the Presidency, Exhibiting a Complete View of Our Foreign Relations Since That Time.** 12 vols. 3rd ed. Boston: Thomas B. Waite and Sons, 1819. This collection is usually referred to as *Waite's State Papers*. This also contains selected documents and papers for the period indicated.

A third collection is:

U.S. Congress. **Compilation of the Messages and Papers of the Presidents, 1789–1897.** 10 vols. Washington, D.C., 1896–1899. Each volume covers one or more administrations from Washington's through the second term of Cleveland.

U.S. National Archives and Records Service, General Services Administration. **Your Government's Records in the National Archives.** Washington, D.C.: U.S. Government Printing Office, 1950, pp. 102. (See *Archives of the United States Government.*)

Guides for the Use of Documents

Bemis, Samuel F., and Griffin, Grace G. **Guide to the Diplomatic History of the United States, 1775–1921.** Washington, D.C.: U.S. Government Printing Office, 1935. New York: Peter Smith, 1951, pp. xvii+979. Designed to guide the reader through material, printed and unprinted, concerning the diplomatic history of the U.S. The book is divided into two parts. Part I contains a bibliography arranged topically and chronologically to indicate sources on a particular subject, with brief explanatory comment when necessary, as well as suggestions for further sources in manuscript and archive collections, and for finding of relevant maps. Part II, "Remarks on Sources," contains comments concerning the sources, analyses of printed state papers, some guidance to manuscript material, and suggestions for exploration.

Boyd, Anne Morris. **United States Government Publications.** 3rd ed.

revised by Rae E. Rips. New York: H. W. Wilson Co., 1949, pp. 627. This is a comprehensive treatment of the publications of the Government of the United States. The arrangement is by the branches and their departments and the individual agencies. Under "Department of State" one will find descriptions of its history, organization, and duties. The indexes and bibliographical guides to foreign relations are listed with annotations. Also listed are periodicals and directories, conference series, department and foreign service series, lists of treaties, compilations of treaties, territorial papers, and miscellaneous publications.

Brimmer, Brenda. **A Guide to the Use of United Nations Documents, Including Reference to the Specialized Agencies and Special U.N. Bodies.** Dobbs Ferry, N.Y.: Oceana Publications, 1962, pp. xv+272. (See *International Organizations: United Nations, Selected Documents and Records.*)

Brown, Everett S. **Manual of Government Publications: United States and Foreign.** New York: Appleton-Century-Crofts, Inc., 1950, pp. ix+121. This volume is "limited in scope and designed for practical use" (Preface). It is not intended as a bibliography to political science in general. It is designed to aid the student in using government publications, with emphasis on American and British Governments and the League of Nations and the U.N. The materials are grouped under subject headings, but there is no index. Although it has not been revised since publication in 1950 and consequently lacks recent material, especially in the area of U.N. Documents, it is a useful guide.

Checklist of United States Public Documents, 1789–1909. 3rd ed. rev. & enl. Washington, D.C.: U.S. Government Printing Office, 1911, pp. 1707. The period covered by this edition for Congressional documents is from the 1st to the end of the 60th Congress. The period for departmental publications is from the organization of the U.S. Government to December 31, 1909. It also includes a few publications, not published until 1910 or 1911, which were annual reports or serial publications covering the year 1909. The first editions were issued in 1892 and 1895. Departmental publications are classified alphabetically first by Department or independent publishing office, then by bureaus, offices, or divisions of these two categories, third by series, and fourth, by book numbers. Congressional documents are arranged chronologically. Not to be confused with the *Catalog of Public Documents.*

Great Britain. **Government Publications Monthly List.** London: H.M. Stationery Office, 1922-. "Contains: 1. Parliamentary Publications. 2. Non-parliamentary Publications. 3. Periodicals. 4. Miscellaneous publications . . . Each monthly list is indexed . . . A *Consolidated List of Government Publications* is published at the end of each year and contains an index . . ." Title of the annual list varies. Since 1956 has been titled **Catalogue of Government Publications.** (Brown, p. 53)

Great Britain, Parliament, House of Commons. **General Index to the Bills, Reports, Estimates, Accounts and Papers, Printed by Order of the House of Commons and to the Papers Presented by Command.** London: H.M. Stationery Office, 1853-. In three volumes. Volume I covers the period 1801–1852; Volume II, 1852–1899; Volume III, 1900 to 1948–1949 (published in 1960). The two earlier volumes have an alphabetical and classified list of principal headings. The latest volume is divided into two parts, the first including notes for users of the index (the papers are listed by subject) and the general index. Part Two consists of a list of Short Titles of the Bills.

Leidy, W. Phillip. **A Popular Guide to Government Publications.** 2nd ed. New York and London: Columbia University Press, 1963, pp. 291. The table of contents is arranged in alphabetical and topical order. The following chapters are most pertinent: Atomic Energy, Citizenship, Communism and Fascism, Historic Documents, History, International Affairs, Travel, United States Government, Vital Statistics, World War I, World War II.

List of the Serial Publications of Foreign Governments, 1815–1931. Edited by Winifred Gregory. New York: H. W. Wilson Co., 1932, pp. xii+720. Compiled for the American Council of Learned Societies, American Library Association, and the National Research Council. An attempt to catalog the official publications of foreign governments for the years indicated. The editor indicates that the list is not complete but that its preparation was intended as "a foundation on which to build."

Moor, Carol C., and Chamberlin, Waldo. **How to Use United Nations Documents.** New York: New York University Press, 1952, pp. 26. (See *International Organizations: United Nations, Selected Documents and Records.*)

Official Publications of European Governments. Paris: Reference Service on International Affairs, American Library in Paris, [1926], pp.

259. A bibliography of official material published by European governments. Many of the documents are no longer available. Publications of each government are arranged by ministry. Publications are listed in the language of the government publishing, but the annotations are in English.

Powell, John Harvey. **The Books of a New Nation: United States Government Publications, 1774–1814.** Philadelphia: University of Pennsylvania Press, 1957, pp. 170. A series of lectures delivered by the author, an A. S. W. Rosenbach Fellow in Bibliography, 1956. A bibliographer's discussion of U.S. Government publications for the dates above.

Schmeckebier, Laurence F., and Eastin, Roy B. **Government Publications and Their Use.** Revised edition. Washington, D.C.: Brookings Institution, 1961, pp. 476. It describes the guides to government publications and also evaluates available indexes, catalogs, and bibliographies. Notice pp. 326–355 which deal specifically with foreign affairs, including treaties, executive agreements, diplomatic correspondence, Congressional publications on Foreign Relations, etc.

U.S. Government Publications in Microprint available from Readex Microprint Corporation, 115 University Place, New York 3, N.Y.: (1) **U.S. Government Depository Publications, 1956-.** (2) **U.S. Government Non-Depository Publications, 1953-.** (3) **U.S. Government Serial Set, 1817–1865.** (4) **American State Papers, 1789–1838.**

U.S. Library of Congress, Processing Dept. **Monthly Checklist of State Publications.** Washington, D.C.: U.S. Government Printing Office, 1910-. (See *Guides to Literature.*)

U.S. Office of the Federal Register, National Archives and Records Service, General Services Administration. **United States Government Organization Manual.** Revised. Washington, D.C.: U.S. Government Printing Office, 1935-. Annual. Detailed description of function of each branch of the United States government—Legislative, Judicial, Executive—includes departments, independent agencies, selected boards, committees, and commissions. Also gives supplemental information concerning quasi-official agencies such as National Academy of Sciences, National Research Council, selected multilateral international organizations, selected bilateral organizations, and commonly used abbreviations. Appendix B lists representative publications from all agencies publishing, with descriptions. It is not an order list, however, but complete lists can be obtained from the agencies themselves. Acquaintance with it will help toward understanding of the structure of the U.S. government and therefore the sources of its documents.

U.S. Superintendent of Documents. **Index to the Reports and Documents of Congress with Numerical Lists and Schedule of Volumes.** 43 vols. Washington, D.C.: U.S. Government Printing Office, 1897–1933. This is a "consolidated index" ordered published by act of Congress January 12, 1895. Prior to the 60th Congress, 1st session, the full title of the *Index* was:

Index to the Subjects of the Documents and Reports and to the Committees, Senators and Representatives Presenting Them, with Tables of the Same in Numerical Order.

This set comprises the index to papers which are printed, by order of Congress, separately from the *Congressional Record* and which do not appear in the *Record*, but which appear numbered consecutively in four series: *Senate Documents, Reports of Senate Committees, House Documents,* and *Reports of House Committees.* Sometimes the four series are referred to as the *Congressional Serial Set.*

In this *Index* each document or report can be found under its subject or subjects, under the Committee, if any, which prepared it, or under the name of the Senator, Representative, or Delegate who presented it.

The *Documents Index* is not to be confused with the *Record Index* which is an index to the *Congressional Record,* the report of the daily proceedings of Congress. Nor is the *Documents Index* to be confused with the *Document Catalog,* which is much wider in scope (see below).

Discontinued by ruling of the Joint Committee on Printing, *Document Index,* No. 43, covering the 72nd Congress, 2nd session, was the last issue. However, numerical lists and schedules of volumes were included in the *Document Catalog* until September 1947. At that time inclusion of the contents of bound volumes of the *Congressional Serial Set* in the *Monthly Catalog* (again see below) was discontinued, but the House and Senate Documents and Reports are arranged in checklist order as they are published each month in the *Monthly Catalog* under the headings of House of Representatives and Senate.

U.S. Superintendent of Documents. **United States Government Publications: Monthly Catalog.** Washington, D.C.: U.S. Government Printing Office, 1941-. This has been issued in monthly form since January,

1941, giving current publications of all branches of the Government. The December issue each year contains an annual index, and the monthly issues are bound every six months into permanent volumes. There is a cumulative index published every ten years. During the ten-year period should titles of publications have changed, a compromise subject heading is used to cover the publication. Each monthly catalog also contains an author and subject index. Prior to publication in this form the U.S. Superintendent of Documents published the *Document Catalog,* whose complete title is as follows:

U.S. Superintendent of Documents. **Catalog of the Public Documents of Congress and of All Departments of the Government of the United States for the Period March 4, 1893—December 31, 1940.** 25 vols. Washington, D.C.: U.S. Government Printing Office, 1896–1945.

This form of cataloging the public documents of the Government was provided for by Congress in an act approved January 12, 1895. This work includes all of the government publications and is not to be confused with the *Document Index,* a companion work which covers only documents numbered in the *Congressional Serial Set.*

All entries in the *Catalog,* whether author, subject, or title, are in a single alphabetical arrangement. Departments, bureaus, offices, divisions, commissions, surveys, etc. are treated as authors. Beginning with the 60th Congress, documents as well as reports are numbered through the Congress, whereas, prior to that time, Senate and House documents began a new set of numbers with each session, although committee reports were numbered for the whole Congress without regard to sessions. Publications of bureaus are under the name of the bureau, but a scientific or literary publication by a bureau chief is listed under his own name.

There have been variations in methods of listing reports of Congressional standing committees. Beginning with the 54th Congress, 1st session, the reports are listed under the names of the committees and under the subject but, beginning with Vol. 11, the 62nd session of Congress, committee reports can be found under the title of the bill or joint resolution or under the subject matter if there is no title. Methods of referring to private bills have also varied throughout the years. In the earlier volumes references to private bills can be found under the names of the claimants. In later editions private pension bills can be found under "Pensions," but not under the name of the claimant; in still later editions it is necessary to consult the session indexes of the Congressional Record under the name of the individual claimant in order to trace a private bill.

This form of cataloging government publications was preceded by:

Ames, John Griffith. **Comprehensive Index to the Publications of the United States Government, 1881–1893.** 2 vols. Washington, D.C.: U.S. Government Printing Office, 1905. Compiled in compliance with a House and Senate joint resolution in order that an index might be made of all the publications of the U.S. Government from 1881, the termination date of the *Descriptive Catalog of Government Publications* by Benjamin P. Poore, to 1883, the date the U.S. Superintendent of Documents' *Document Catalog* commences. The *Index* is arranged with the left-hand column showing the origin (the Department or office, the Committee of Senate or House, or the author) of the documents, the right-hand column showing the classification, with a central column describing the subject. The *Index* is arranged alphabetically according to subject. This *Index* is not to be confused with the *Documents Index*.

The earliest of the catalogs for United States government documents is:

Poore, Benjamin Perley. **A Descriptive Catalogue of the Government Publications of the United States, September 5, 1774—March 4, 1881.** Compiled by order of Congress. Washington, D.C.: U.S. Government Printing Office, 1885, pp. 1392. Gives the title of each book, pamphlet, or document; the author's name; date of publication; a brief summary of contents; the number of pages; the series in which the publication may be found (for example: Senate Papers, 14th Congress, 1st session).

This series of catalogs of government publications is not to be confused with the *Checklist of U.S. Public Documents 1789–1909.*

Ward, Robert E., *et al.* **Studying Politics Abroad: Field Research in the Developing Areas.** Boston and Toronto: Little, Brown and Company, 1964, pp. viii + 245. This is a splendid paperback source book combining the suggestions of experienced scholars concerning the problems of doing research in developing areas. The contents deal with: (a) developing areas: problems for research, (b) the research environment, (c) common problems in field research, (d) documentary research, (e) political interviewing, (f) survey techniques, (g) research design. Equally valuable are the Appendices which enumerate specifically (a) documentary research facilities in some developing countries, (b) Western European sources of documentation on developing areas, (c) United States sources of documentation on developing countries, (d) newspaper sources in the principal developing countries, (e) selected bibliography of bibliographies and documentary sources. Most important is Appendix A, which enumerates and describes National Libraries and National Archives in developing countries.

Encyclopedias

The number of national encyclopedias is voluminous. Encyclopedias are published in Austria, Canada, France, Germany, Great Britain, Italy, Spain, the Soviet Union, Switzerland, and the United States, among other countries. Listed here is the *Encyclopedia of the Social Sciences,* of special importance in the field of International Relations, as well as several less well-known.

The Encyclopaedia of Islam: A Dictionary of the Geography, Ethnography, and Biography of the Muhammadan Peoples. 4 vols. and Supplement. Leyden: Brill; London: Luzac, 1911–1938. A new edition of this work is in preparation, Vol. I having been published in 1960, Vol. II in 1961. The new edition has the title, *The Encyclopedia of Islam.* The work has been completed by a number of leading Orientalists under the patronage of the International Union of Academies. More space is given in the new edition to economic and social topics, and there are more cross-references in English and French to facilitate the use of the work by non-Orientalists. Bibliographies are included with most articles, and the articles are detailed and scholarly.

Encyclopaedia of the Social Sciences. Editor-in-Chief, E. R. A. Seligman; Associate Editor, Alvin Johnson. 15 vols. New York and London: Macmillan, 1930–1935. The introduction discusses and defines, for purposes of the encyclopedia, social sciences and "semi-social sciences." For the social sciences—politics, economics, law, anthropology, sociology, penology, and social work—the editors endeavored to include all the important topics of these disciplines. In the case of the semi-social sciences, defined as ethics, education, philosophy, and psychology, the editors aimed to select those topics of which social aspects were becoming increasingly important. This was also true, but to a more limited degree, of biology, geography, medicine, philology, and art. The work combines characteristics of a dictionary and a handbook. The topics are arranged alphabetically, without regard to length, and there is a thorough system of cross-references.

All articles are by scholars. A new *Encyclopaedia* is scheduled to appear in 1966.

Staatslexikon: Recht, Wirtschaft, Gesellschaft. Hrsg. von der Görres-Gesellschaft zur Pflege der Wissenschaft im Katholischen Deutschland. 6. völlig neu. bearb. und erw. Aufl. Freiburg: Herder, 1957-. "First published 1887; 5th ed. 1926–32 (5 v.). The 6th ed. (v. 1–6 [1959–61]: A-SCHWEIZ) is to be in 8 volumes with 4,000 signed articles. Systematic and lengthy treatment of subjects from the Catholic viewpoint; bibliographies appended to articles. Of particular interest are the articles on the Federal Republic of Germany, Ghana, and Communism. Biographies are included (e.g. of Gandhi, Hitler); that of Karl Marx (1. Life; 2. Appreciation) has 3 columns of text and nearly one column of bibliography. The 6-column article on Laos has a bibliography of items up to 1958." (Walford, 1963 Supplement, p. 47)

Theimer, Walter. **An Encyclopedia of Modern World Politics.** New York: Rinehart and Co., 1950, pp. 696. "Expansion of this author's *Penguin Political Dictionary,* which was published in England in 1939 with the cover title, 'An ABC of International Affairs,' German and Danish. The new volume, prepared especially for American readers, gives wider coverage to American politics. A survey of 'political terms, systems, trends, problems, and watchwords of the contemporary world,' it is alphabetically arranged in dictionary style with brief explanations, held in most cases to a single paragraph, of each name or phrase. It includes short political sketches of almost all countries, and a few biographical notes on outstanding political figures. Problems to which special attention is given are those of the spring of 1949." (Conover, p. 54)

The Universal Jewish Encyclopedia: An Authoritative and Popular Presentation of Jews and Judaism Since the Earliest Times. 10 vols., reading guide and index. New York: The Universal Jewish Encyclopedia, Inc., 1939–1944. These 10 volumes were conceived as a means of providing comprehensive, scientific, and concise information concerning Jewish History and Christian-Jewish relations, in order to combat anti-Semitism with education. More than 10,000 articles are included. There are among these biographies, some with references to persons other than Jews, who have been connected with Jewish history.

Worldmark Encyclopedia of the Nations: A Practical Guide to the Geographic, Historical, Political, Social, and Economic Status of All

Nations, Their International Relationships, and the United Nations System. New York: Worldmark Press; Harper and Brothers, 1960, pp. 4156. The first part of the work deals with countries individually in all aspects of their national life, historical background, commerce, education, etc. in order to give a comprehensive picture of the culture of each nation. Part Two deals with the United Nations system, with articles on each of its bodies and agencies.

Films: Guides

Institutions such as the University of Indiana, University of
Southern California, University of Michigan, and Columbia University have large collections of films which are rented or loaned
to other institutions. Each of these above-mentioned universities
has a catalog to its own collection of films.

American Historical Association. **Guide to Photocopied Historical Materials in the United States and Canada.** Edited by Richard W. Hale,
Jr. Ithaca, N.Y.: Cornell University Press, 1961, pp. xxxiv+241.
This volume was sponsored by the American Historical Association
and was designed to provide basic bibliographical information on
photocopied manuscripts of interest to historians available in
depositories in the U.S. and Canada. For reproductions of published
materials the *Guide* lists only finding aids, but a union list of holdings
of bodies of historical manuscripts in photocopy forms the major
part of this work since these materials are not generally covered by
finding aids.

**A Catalog of Files and Microfilms of the German Foreign Ministry
Archives 1920–1945.** 2 vols. Compiled and edited by George O.
Kent. Stanford, California: The Hoover Institution on War, Revolution, and Peace, Stanford University, 1962. Published as a joint
project of the United States Department of State and the Hoover
Institution on War, Revolution, and Peace, this catalog lists all the
files from the political archives of the German Foreign Ministry for
the period indicated, which were seized at the end of World War
II by the American and British armies, indicating the files which have
been microfilmed and where the microfilms can be found. There is
also a list of unfilmed material in the Archive of the German Foreign
Office in Bonn. This is a continuation of the *Catalog of German
Foreign Ministry Files and Microfilms, 1867–1920,* published by the
American Historical Association in 1959.

Educational Film Guide. New York: H. W. Wilson Co., 1936–1962.
Annual with cumulative monthly supplements. Earlier title was *Educational Film Catalog.* Films for classrooms, libraries, etc. are listed

alphabetically and by subject in Part I. In Part II brief descriptions of the films are given.

Guide to Microforms in Print. Edited by Albert James Diaz. Washington, D.C.: Microcard Editions, Inc., 1961-. Annual. A comprehensive guide to materials available from U.S. publishers on microfilm or other microform. It lists only the publications for sale on a regular basis. Includes books (listed alphabetically by author), journals and sets (listed by title), newspapers (listed by state, city, name), archival materials and manuscripts, projects (such as bibliographies).

Newspapers on Microfilm. 5th ed. Compiled under direction of George A. Schwegmann, Jr. Washington, 1963, pp. xv+305. (See *Newspapers: Directories* [*Worldwide*].)

NSDAP Hauptarchiv: Guide to the Hoover Institution Microfilm Collection. Compiled by Grete Heinz and Agnes F. Peterson. Stanford, California: The Hoover Institution on War, Revolution, and Peace, Stanford University, 1964, pp. 175. "The Guide lists the content of 134 reels of microfilm containing the records of the Nazi Party Central Archives. It gives reel numbers, folder titles in German, and a brief description of the contents in English. A name and organization index is appended. The archive was microfilmed at the U.S. Document Center in Berlin from where the actual documents have now been returned to the German authorities. Two smaller collections containing Streicher and Himmler materials have also been included." (Agnes F. Peterson, co-author)

Philadelphia Bibliographical Center and Union Library Catalogue, Committee on Microphotography. **Union List of Microfilms: Cumulation 1949–1959.** 2 vols. Ann Arbor, Michigan: J. W. Edwards, 1961. These volumes are the final publication of the *Union List of Microfilms,* published since 1942, this being the last of 3 cumulated lists. About 52,000 entries for accessions from 215 libraries in the U.S. and Canada are reported, for July 1, 1949 through July 31, 1959. The companion volume is *Union List of Microfilms, Revised, Enlarged and Cumulated Edition,* 1951. Useful as a guide to locating microfilmed material, except newspapers (in *Newspapers on Microfilm*), theses (in *Dissertation Abstracts*), manuscripts (from Library of Congress). Each entry contains all the bibliographical detail obtainable, as well as location of master negatives, negatives, and positives.

Subject Guide to Microforms in Print. Edited by Albert James Diaz. Washington, D.C.: Microcard Editions, Inc., 1962-. A guide by subject classification to materials available on microfilm and other microforms. Complements *Guide to Microforms in Print,* which lists materials in alphabetic order. Lists are for U.S. publishers only.

U.S. Library of Congress. **Library of Congress Catalog—Motion Pictures and Filmstrips: A Cumulative List of Works Represented by Library of Congress Printed Cards.** Washington, D.C.: 1953-. Quarterly. Title varies: 1953, *Library of Congress Catalog—Films.* Issued in three quarterly numbers and annual cumulation. "Includes entries for all motion pictures and filmstrips (but not for microfilms) currently catalogued on L.C. printed cards . . . attempting to cover all educational motion pictures and filmstrips released in the United States and Canada and all current theatrical motion pictures which are copyrighted in the United States." (Introduction)

U.S. Library of Congress. **National Register of Microfilm Masters.** (In preparation.) Will record the location of master negatives of microcopies of books and periodicals, both in the U.S. and abroad. It will be a supplement of the L.C.'s *National Union Catalog.*

U.S. National Archives and Records Service, General Services Administration. **List of National Archives Microfilm Publications.** Washington, D.C.: U.S. Government Printing Office, 1961, pp. 231. (See *Archives of the United States Government.*)

Guides to Literature

American Historical Association. **Guide to Historical Literature.** New York: Macmillan, 1961, pp. 962. A bibliography of selected historical material, with annotations, organized by political and geographical areas, with further division under each area according to type of literature, i.e., documents, histories, bibliographies, etc. It follows an earlier work prepared by the Committee on Bibliography of the American Historical Association in cooperation with the American Library Association, *Guide to Historical Literature,* edited by Matthew Dutcher *et al.* (New York: Macmillan, 1931), but does not entirely replace it because some earlier material has been deleted.

Bemis, Samuel F., and Griffin, Grace G. **Guide to the Diplomatic History of the United States, 1775–1921.** Washington, D.C.: U.S. Government Printing Office, 1935. New York: Peter Smith, 1951, pp. xvii+979. (See *Documents: Guides for the Use of Documents.*)

Guide to Reference Material. Edited by Arthur J. Walford. London: The Library Association, 1959, pp. viii+543. Supplement, 1963, pp. vii+370. The original *Guide* lists and describes approximately 3,000 selected reference books and bibliographies in the fields of philosophy, psychology, social sciences, science and technology, geography, history, biography, mathematics and applied sciences, among others. The supplement continues the same arrangement, adding new works in these fields, and includes three new fields—genealogy and heraldry, ancient times and medieval and modern history.

Lewis, Peter R. **The Literature of the Social Sciences: An Introductory Survey and Guide.** London: The Library Association, 1960, pp. 222. Deals with sources in the social sciences from approximately 1800 to the end of 1958, with emphasis on the twentieth century. There is no subject index, and the form of the organization makes the book rather difficult to use. Major chapter headings include "Economic History and Conditions," "Economic History, Great Britain," "Political Science and Public Administration," "Law," "International Affairs," "Sociology."

Maichel, Karol. **Guide to Russian Reference Books.** Vol. I: **General Bibliographies and Reference Books.** Edited by J. S. G. Simmons.

Stanford, California: The Hoover Institution on War, Revolution, and Peace, Stanford University, 1962, pp. 92. This is the first volume of the 6-volume set. The forthcoming volumes will be: Vol. II, Historical Sciences; Vol. III, Social Sciences, Religion and Philosophy; Vol. IV, Humanities; Vol. V, Science, Technology and Medicine; Vol. VI, Supplementary Materials and Cumulative Index. Meticulous and remarkable. A very useful source.

Schmeckebier, Laurenc F., and Eastin, Roy B.. **Government Publications and Their Use.** Revised edition. Washington, D.C.: The Brookings Institution, 1961, pp. 476. (See *Documents: Guides for the Use of Documents.*)

United Nations Educational, Scientific, and Cultural Organization. **Bibliographical Services throughout the World.** Paris: UNESCO, 1951/53-. Annual. "Reports on the activities of countries and international organizations in the field of national bibliographies, union lists, library cooperation, periodicals lists and indexes, and related fields; many useful lists of bibliographies, but coverage is uneven." (Walford, p. 3) No index. Kept up-to-date by Unesco's *Bibliography, Documentation, Terminology.*

U.S. Library of Congress, General Reference and Bibliography Division. **A Guide to Bibliographic Tools for Research in Foreign Affairs.** Compiled by Helen F. Conover. 2nd ed. Washington, 1958, pp. iii+145+15-page supplement. 1st edition 1956. The 2nd edition adds a 15-page supplement. An excellent annotated bibliography, with 292 main entries and much other material referred to in the annotations. "It contains bibliographies, manuals, indexes, surveys, and other publications of value to the American librarian or student doing preliminary research on the political and economic scene abroad. . . . Preference has been given to sources in the English language, although some foreign language material has been considered indispensable." (Foreword)

U.S. Library of Congress, Processing Dept. **Monthly Checklist of State Publications.** Washington, D.C.: U.S. Government Printing Office, 1910-. A bibliography of publications of states, territories, and possessions of the U.S. received by the Library of Congress. There is an annual index to both subjects and titles.

White, Carl M., and associates. **Sources of Information in the Social Sciences: A Guide to the Literature.** Totowa, N.J.: The Bedminster Press, 1964, pp. xiii+498. For the purposes of this guide, the authors have divided the social sciences into seven disciplines: history, economics and business administration, sociology, anthropology, psychology, education, and political science. "For each subject, the treatment falls into two parts. First a specialist, sought out for his grasp of the literature, presents a bibliographical review of basic monographic works for a collection of substantive material. This review is followed by a list of reference works. Informative annotations are provided for all works except those adequately explained by the title. Specialized works are included, especially when they exemplify types of sources important for reference purposes." (Preface, pp. ix–x) The contributions are all signed. The most important works are indexed.

Winchell, C. M. **Guide to Reference Books.** 7th ed. Chicago: American Library Association, 1951, pp. xvii+645. 4 Supplements. Supplements 1950–1952; 1953–1955; 1956–1958; 1959–June 1962. First published in 1902. "The authoritative work on reference books. The 7th ed. and its supplements cover some 7,500 works. Arrangement is systematic, by disciplines, the general material (Bibliography; Libraries; Societies; Encyclopedias; Periodicals and newspapers; Government documents; Dissertations) preceding the subject classes, which are roughly in Dewey order. Annotations are excellent, although they are not uniformly provided. The scope is international, with less emphasis on Scandinavia. Applied science receives less attention than the social sciences and literature." (Walford, p. 26)

Institutions in the Field of International Relations

American Agencies Interested in International Affairs. Compiled by Ruth Savord and Donald Wasson. New York: Council on Foreign Relations, 1955, pp. vii+289. Gives information concerning organizations engaged in research, action groups, a few international organizations whose work is centered in the U.S., and organizations of exiles working for freedom of their countries. Data is partial or complete for 363 organizations. Includes personnel index.

Carnegie Endowment for International Peace. **Institutes of International Affairs.** New York: 1953, pp. 131. "Handbook listing and describing institutes of world affairs which have risen in many countries 'following the pattern set by the Royal Institute in London and the Council for Foreign Relations in New York in 1919.' The booklet begins with a summary of the development of the institute movement, and the second part describes individual institutes, their policies, programs and problems. Thirty-five institutes in twenty or so countries are discussed in detail. In most cases, publications of the institutes are mentioned." (Conover, p. 42)

The Eastern European Academies of Science: A Directory. Prepared by The Office of the Foreign Secretary, National Academy of Sciences-National Research Council, 1963, pp. v+148. Annotated outlines of academies of sciences for the countries of Bulgaria, Czechoslovakia, Hungary, Poland, Rumania, and Yugoslavia. Listing includes brief history of each academy, its current organization, responsibilities, titles of its main periodicals, rosters of leading academic officials, affiliated institutes, and their directors, plus biographical sketches of prominent academicians in each country. (Preface, p. iii)

The Foundation Directory: Edition 2. Edited by Ann D. Walton and Marianna O. Lewis. Prepared by The Foundation Library Center. New York: Russell Sage Foundation, 1964, pp. 1,000. Edition 1 published in 1960. Contains a selected list of foundations divided into five classes: general research foundations, special purpose foundations, community foundations, company-sponsored foundations, and family foundations. Includes descriptions, when known, of donor, purpose and activities, financial data, and officers.

Index Generalis: General Yearbook of Universities and Educational Institutions, Academies, Archives, Libraries, Scientific Institutes, Botanical and Zoological Gardens, Museums, Observatories, Learned Societies. Paris: Dunod, 1920-. "Besides currency, it has the advantage over its counterpart, *Minerva* . . . that it comprises within one cover the entire world of scholarship. Section 5, the academies and societies, is classed by nature of the research work, agriculture, anthropology, archaeology, etc. Details given for each institution include name and address, usually a note of general information, list of directors, principal professors, etc." (Conover, pp. 50–51)

Olzog, Günter, ed. **Das Studium der Politischen Wissenschaften im In- und Ausland.** Munich: Isar Verlag, 1953, pp. 156. "A catalog of universities and institutions specializing in the study of political sciences in 34 countries. . . . No Eastern European countries are included." (Conover, p. 44)

International Conferences
and Congresses

Gregory, Winifred, ed. **International Congresses and Conferences, 1840–1937: A Union List of their Publications Available in Libraries of the United States and Canada.** New York: H. W. Wilson Co., 1938, pp. 229. "Excludes diplomatic conferences and congresses, and those held under the auspices of the League of Nations. Entries arranged alphabetically. Indicates libraries where publications may be found." (Brown, p. 112) Subject index. Includes unofficial reports.

International Associations. Brussels: Union of International Associations, 1949-. (See *International Organizations: Other.*)

U.S. Dept. of State, Division of International Conferences. **Participation of the United States Government in International Conferences including the Composition of United States Delegations and Summaries of the Proceedings.** Washington, D.C.: U.S. Government Printing Office, 1931/32-. Annual. Title varies. "Yearbook reviewing the international conferences to which American delegations have been sent, including for each conference the names of the delegation, the list of other countries participating, and a short statement of agenda and recommendations." (Conover, p. 65)

International Law

The American Journal of International Law. Washington, D.C.: American Society of International Law, 1907-. With Supplements.

The British Yearbook of International Law. London: Oxford University Press, 1920-. Annual. Not published 1939–1943. This yearbook "deals with public and private international law. It contains articles, notes, case notes and book reviews of a very high standard." (Walford, p. 124)

Dictionnaire de la Terminologie du Droit International. Publié sous le patronage de l'Union Académique Internationale. Paris: Sirey, 1960, pp. xv+755. (See *Dictionaries*.)

Geneva Research Centre. **Répertoire des questions de droit international général posées devant la Societé des Nations, 1920–1940.** Compiled by Walter Shiffer. Geneva: 1942, pp. 390. "Compiled chiefly in the French language. . . . English equivalents are given for titles and subtitles, the table of contents, and the alphabetical index." (Editorial Note, p. 1) Intended for students of international law in order to make materials more readily available, it digests the rules of international law erected by the League of Nations.

Hackworth, Green Haywood. **Digest of International Law.** 8 vols. Washington, D.C.: U.S. Government Printing Office, 1940–1944. Follows, in general, the outline of Moore's Digest, but does not duplicate its material. According to its compiler, "For the most part the Digest represents the position of the Government of the United States on the subjects discussed as revealed by the voluminous records of the Department of State . . ." Vol. I, Chapter I is a general discussion of International Law, Chapter II defines some terminology frequently used. The remainder of Vol. I and the following volumes through Vol. VII consider various aspects of International Law. Vol. VIII consists of a General Index and a List of Cases.

Haensch, Günther. **Internationale Terminologie: Diplomatie, Verträge, Internationale Organisationen, Konferenzen . . .** Stuttgart: Müller, 1954, pp. 180. (See *Dictionaries*.)

Harvard University, Law School, Library. **Annual Legal Bibliography.** Cambridge, Mass.: 1960/61-. With its supplement, *Current Legal*

Bibliography, the cumulative *Annual Legal Bibliography* makes available "quick and accurate information about new legal publications . . . a ready current bibliography for those who are primarily interested in Anglo-American law . . . [and] . . . as a guide not heretofore available to legal writing in many parts of the world." (Preface, Vol. I, 1961, p. v) See Sections C, D, and E, Private International Law, Public International Law, and International Economic and Social Affairs respectively.

International Committee of Comparative Law. **Catalogue des Sources de Documentation Juridique dans le Monde** [A Register of Legal Documentation in the World]. Paris: UNESCO, 1953, pp. 362. Bibliography which lists legal periodicals from 84 countries.

The International and Comparative Law Quarterly. London: British Institute of International and Comparative Law, 1952-.

International Court of Justice. Publications of the International Court of Justice follow the pattern established by the Permanent Court of International Justice. They are considered U.N. Publications. They are published by the Registry of the Court in The Netherlands, and are sold in the United States by International Documents Service, Columbia University Press, New York.

Series A is titled **Reports of Judgments, Advisory Opinions and Others.** It contains the Reports of the decisions of the Court in French and English. Decisions are published unbound separately as rendered, and bound yearly.

In Series B, **Pleadings, Oral Arguments, Documents,** volumes containing all the documents in each case, including speeches of counsel, and pleadings and all evidence, are published after each case. Short title: *ICJ Pleadings.*

Series C, **Acts and Documents Concerning the Organization of the Court** (1 volume, 2nd edition, 1947; short title: *ICJ Organization*) contains the text of the Charter of the U.N. in English and French, Statute of the Court, and Rules of the Court.

Series D, **Yearbook** (short title: *ICJ Yearbook*) began publication in 1947. The annual edition covers the period from July 16 of the preceding year to July 15 of the current year. The French edition is titled *Annuaire.* This is a continuation of the *Annual Report* of the Permanent Court and also contains a Bibliography which is reprinted separately annually as *Bibliography of the International Court of Justice.* This is a comprehensive list of the publications of the International Court of Justice, containing a table of contents, alphabetical index of authors' names and of names cited, and an alphabetic index of subjects. The indexes are cumulative.

A series has been reserved for the publication of treaties or relevant extracts providing for the jurisdiction of the Court. It is to be titled **Collection of Texts Governing the Jurisdiction of the Court** (short title: *ICJ Jurisdiction*). This information has been included in Chapter X of each *Yearbook*.

A **Catalogue** of the publications of the Court is published, which is brought up to date annually. An addendum is issued for the years in which a new edition is not published.

International Law Reports. Edited by H. Lauterpacht and E. Lauterpacht. London: Butterworth and Co., 1940-. A continuation of a series, the first 16 volumes of which were titled *Annual Digest and Reports of Public International Law Cases.* The series began with the year 1919, and to date 28 volumes have been published covering selected decisions of international and national courts and tribunals through 1959. Decisions are arranged in current volumes under the following headings: International Law in General, States as International Persons, State Territory, Jurisdiction, State Responsibility, The Individual in International Law, Diplomatic and Consular Intercourse and Privileges, Treaties, International Organization and Administration, Disputes, War and Neutrality.

Moore, John Bassett. **Digest of International Law.** 8 vols. Washington: U.S. Government Printing Office, 1906. The full title also describes the work: "A digest of international law as embodied in diplomatic discussions, treaties and other international agreements, international awards, the decisions of municipal courts, and writings of jurists, and especially in documents, published and unpublished, issued by presidents and secretaries of state of the United States, the opinions of the attorneys-general, and the decisions of courts, federal and state." This work was preceded by the *Digest of the International Law of the United States,* edited by Francis Wharton, LL.D., published in 3 volumes in 1886, with a second issue incorporating new material in the 3rd volume in 1887. The present work follows the same plan as Wharton's *Digest.* The first seven volumes consist of the digest; the eighth is devoted to a general index and list of documents. Chapter I, Vol. I is devoted to a general history and discussion of International Law; the rest of the work deals with specific questions, categorized by chapter headings.

Price, Miles O., and Bitner, Harry. **Effective Legal Research.** Student

Edition Revised. Boston and Toronto: Little, Brown and Co., 1962, pp. xx+496. Designed for students, this volume, revised for that purpose, contains a chapter titled Treaties and Other International Acts of the United States, giving concise information as to forms of publication for treaties and executive agreements; lists and subject indexes of international acts; procedures for research in international acts.

Publications of the Permanent Court of International Justice. Leyden: A. W. Sijthoff, 1922–1946. "These publications were issued in French and English in the following series: Series A, **Collection of Judgments.** Series B, **Collection of Advisory Opinions.** Series A/B, **Collection of Judgments, Orders and Advisory Opinions.** (On February 21, 1931, the Court adopted a new version of its rules and combined Series A and Series B.) Series C, **Pleadings, Oral Statements and Documents.** Series D, **Acts and Documents Concerning the Organization of the Court.** Series E, **Annual Reports.** (Each report contains a 'Bibliographical List of Official and Unofficial Publications Concerning the Permanent Court of International Justice.') [See separate reference.] Series Γ, **General Indexes** (issued twice during each period of nine years, alternately at intervals of five and four years)." (Brown, p. 102)

Permanent Court of International Justice. **Annual Report.** 1st to 15th. Leyden: A. W. Sijthoff, 1925–1939. Each volume contains a Bibliographical List of official and unofficial reports concerning The Court. (See reference below.)

Permanent Court of International Justice. **Bibliographical List of Official and Unofficial Publications Concerning the Court of International Justice.** 2nd ed. Prepared by J. Doumia. The Hague, 1926, pp. 159. With Supplements; 1927–1940/45. Indexes, authors and subjects are cumulated. Reprinted from *Annual Reports,* Series E. (See above.)

Permanent Court of International Justice. **General Indexes.** Leyden: A. W. Sijthoff, 1927–1936. In French and English. There are 3 series in the first General Index. 7 vols. in Series A. Series B consists of 13 vols., and Series C of 12 vols. These 3 series cover sessions 1–11 (1922–1926). The 2nd General Index, also with Series A, B, and C, covers sessions 12th–19th (1927–1930). Series A consists of 16 vols.; B, 4 vols.; C, 6 vols. The 3rd *General Index* consists of Series A/B and C, covering the 20th–35th sessions from 1931–1935. Series A/B has 25 vols. and C has 25 vols.

Satow, Sir Ernest Mason. **A Guide to Diplomatic Practice.** 2nd & rev.
ed. London, New York [etc.]: Longmans, Green & Co., 1922.
"Diplomatic privileges and practices, the classification of diplomatic
agents, the position of Sovereigns and of property owned by them in
foreign countries, the framework of treaties and conventions, ratifi-
cations, and other subjects treated of in the following chapters, may
be considered as forming a part of International Law, and most
treatises on that science deal with them. But it was thought that their
fuller discussion might be of practical utility, not only to members of
the services, but also to the general public and to writers who occupy
themselves with international affairs. Hence the origin of the present
work, believed to be the earliest of its kind published in England."
(Preface, p. vii)

Strupp, Karl. **Wörterbuch des Völkerrechts.** 2. Aufl. hrsg. von Hans-
Jürgen Schlochauer. Berlin: de Gruyter, 1960-. (In progress.) A dictionary of international law, giving signed, comprehensive, documented treatment of cases. Volume I covers A–H. The series is not
yet complete. Volume II is to cover cases from I–R and Volume III,
cases from S–Z.

U.S. Naval War College. **General Index to International Law Situations, Topics, Discussions, Documents, and Decisions.** 30 vols.
Washington, D.C.: U.S. Government Printing Office, 1901–1930.
These volumes cover the years indicated. Annual volumes have individual titles.

Whiteman, Marjorie M. **Digest of International Law.** 2 vols. Washington, D.C.: Department of State, 1963. This is the successor to Hackworth's *Digest of International Law,* and treats public international
law and related matters, especially for the past two decades.

Zagayko, Florence Ferner. **"Guide to a Basic Library on International
Law,"** *Law Library Journal,* Vol. LIII, No. 2 (May 1960), pp. 118–
128. A supplementary guide to existing bibliographies for the purpose of building an international law collection—primarily of reference works and recent publications. Supplements G. P. Speeckaert,
International Institutions and International Organization (see *International Organizations: Other* at Union of International Associations) and U.N., *List of Treaty Collections* (see *Treaty Collections*).

International Organizations

League of Nations

Aufricht, Hans. **Guide to League of Nations Publications: A Bibliographical Survey of the Work of the League, 1920–1947.** New York: Columbia University Press, 1951, pp. xix+682. Covers the entire period of the League from 1920 until the end in 1947, and includes all types of documents, both those on sale and those not included in the sales catalogs, but it is selective, and publications of only passing interest were eliminated, while special attention is given to those documents considered basic. Documents of the principal autonomous organs of the League, i.e., the Permanent Court, the International Labor Organization, etc., are included. Publications of the principal organs are covered as well as the organization of the League, its main activities, major publications, official and unofficial. There are appendixes containing League and U.N. documents.

Breycha-Vauthier, Arthur Carl von. **Sources of Information: A Handbook on the Publications of the League of Nations.** London: Allen & Unwin; New York: Columbia University Press, 1939, pp. 118. This edition has been revised and brought up to December 1, 1938 from earlier editions. (It was first published in German, in 1934, and was followed by Czech, Russian, and French editions.) It was intended to provide a selective guide to materials available in League of Nations publications for students and researchers. It is not a catalogue of the League's publications. (A comprehensive checklist of these publications is provided in Marie G. Carroll's *Key to League of Nations Documents.*) Materials are listed and described concerning problems in the field of international relations, economics, law and social problems, and there are also materials relevant to the domestic problems of national states. Some of the chapter headings are Assembly, Council (Periodical Publications on Political Questions); The League's Activity and Organization of the Secretariat (Descriptive Publications); Social and Humanitarian Work; Political Activities; etc.

71

Carroll, Marie Juliette. **Key to League of Nations Documents Placed on Public Sale, 1920–1929.** Boston: World Peace Foundation, 1930, pp. 340. 4 Supplements. The supplements cover the period from 1930 through 1936, and are followed by mimeographed lists. "The lists of documents . . . are arranged chronologically and serve as a retrospective bibliography of League publications. The first supplement, for 1930, contains a subject index of document titles in the *Key* and in the supplement. All later supplements contain the subject index." (Brown, p. 100)

League of Nations. **Catalogue of Publications, 1920–1935.** Geneva: 1935. 5 Supplements, 1936–1945. "Lists all publications offered for sale to the end of May, 1935. The table of contents and alphabetical index can be used to assist in checking League documents. The explanatory notes for each division are valuable for bibliographical purposes." (Brown, p. 101)

League of Nations. **Treaty Series: Publication of Treaties and International Engagements Registered with the Secretariat of the League.** Vols. 1–205. (Treaty No. 1-4834) Sept. 1920–1944/46. London: Harrison, 1920–1946. (See *Treaty Collections.*)

League of Nations Library. **Brief Guide to the League of Nations Publications.** Revised ed. Geneva: 1930, pp. 32. "An excellent brief official description of League publications. In addition to giving an account of the publications, it describes the system of classification by subjects. It is printed in French and English." (Brown, p. 100)

League of Nations Secretariat, Information Section. **Essential Facts About the League of Nations.** 10th ed. rev. Geneva: Information Section, League of Nations, 1939, pp. 359. "The Covenant of the League of Nations": pp. 11–29. Gives a brief description of the League and its activities.

League of Nations Secretariat, Information Section. **The League from Year to Year.** Geneva: Information Section, League of Nations, 1927/28–1938. This was an annual publication covering the period from Oct., 1926, to 1938. It is analogous to the *Yearbook of the United Nations.* The first of the series has the title, *The League of Nations from Year to Year.* Oct., 1926—Oct., 1927, published in 1928.

League of Nations Secretariat, Information Section. **Monthly Summary of the League of Nations.** Geneva: 1921–1940. "This was a popular survey of the League's work during the preceding month, published in five languages: English, French, German, Italian, and Spanish. It included a calendar of events, a listing of conferences, committees, meetings, etc." Special supplements add to its usefulness. (Aufricht, pp. 117–118) Analogous to the *U.N. Bulletin.*

Ottlik, Georges, ed. **Annuaire de la Société des Nations.** 8 vols. Geneva: Payot et cie., 1927–1938. Not published 1932–1935. "An excellent annual handbook, giving an account of the organization of the League, a historical sketch of its principal activities, the names of member states, relations with nonmember states, an index of persons connected with the League, and a subject index." (Brown, p. 101)

Walters, F. P. **A History of the League of Nations.** 2 vols. New York: Oxford University Press, 1952, pp. 833. Published under the auspices of the Royal Institute of International Affairs. "The standard work of the League of Nations. An objective account. 67 chapters, taking the narrative up to 1946. No bibliography, but a rather general appendix note on sources, v. 2, p. 816–7. Supported by a very good analytical index." (Walford, 1963 Suppl., p. 66)

Watkins, James T., and Robinson, J. William. **General International Organization: A Source Book.** Princeton, N.J.: D. Van Nostrand Co., Inc., 1956, pp. xi+248. (See *International Organizations: United Nations, Selected Documents and Records.*)

United Nations: Activities and General Information

Locating United Nations documents and publications can be simplified by consulting several basic guides. These sources will help the student relate the classification of the publications to the structure of the U.N. and its specialized agencies, making more comprehensible the vast amount of material available. The most important are:

United Nations Documents Index (See *Selected Documents and Records*)
United Nations Publications, 1945–1963: A Reference Catalogue (See *Guides to Publications*)
Brimmer, *A Guide to the Use of United Nations Documents* (See *Selected Documents and Records*)

Publications of the International Court of Justice are considered U.N. publications, but have been arranged under the subject heading International Law together with publications of the Permanent Court of International Justice by which they are preceded.

The Chronicle of United Nations Activities: Weekly Report. New York: Hasid Publishing Co., 1956–1961. This is no longer published; it was an independent publication having no official connection with the U.N. In some issues it contained Bloc Voting in the General Assembly, as well as brief summaries of U.N. debates, main committee reports, and short reports on items on the agenda. For example, it covered chronologically the Suez crisis.

Everyman's United Nations: The Structure, Functions and Work of the Organization and its Related Agencies during the Years 1945– 1963 and a United Nations Chronology for 1963. 7th ed. New York: United Nations Office of Public Information, 1964, pp. x+638. Intended primarily as a reference work for teachers, students, and general readers, it describes recent crises as well as the role of various technical programs, the specialized agencies, the International Court of Justice, and the International Law Commission.

International Organization. Boston: World Peace Foundation, 1947-. Quarterly. "Devoted to study of the United Nations, the specialized international agencies, and other political, economic, international and regional organizations. Contains some general articles by scholars and officials, but mostly it is devoted to summaries of the various organizations' activities. There is a selected bibliography of secondary materials." (Farber, p. 107)

UNESCO Courier. New York: 1948-. Monthly. "Its primary purpose is to describe and publicize the work of Unesco and the problems and situations that organization is concerned with. Covers in a popular style, with many photographs, the activities and developments in education, science and culture in all nations and areas, in serving as 'a window open on the world.' " (Farber, p. 63)

United Nations. **Yearbook of the United Nations.** Lake Success, N.Y.: United Nations Department of Public Information, 1947-. This annual volume presents the history and developments of the U.N.; deals with the organization of the U.N. and the functions of the General Assembly and the Councils, their procedures, matters considered during the year and their annual reports; discusses political and security questions, economic and social questions, questions concerning non-self-governing territories and the International Trusteeship System. Reports on the specialized agencies, e.g., ILO, UNESCO, WHO, etc., are discussed. Also included are lists of sales agents, Information Centres, lists of illustrations and charts, a roster of the U.N., and a general index.

United Nations, Economic and Social Council. **Catalogue of Economic and Social Projects of the United Nations and the Specialized Agencies.** New York: March 1949-. "Descriptive catalog prepared by the Department of Economic Affairs for the Economic and Social Council. Arranged under the various departments and divisions of U.N. and the specialized agencies, the numbered items explain the projects currently represented in the work programs of the organizations concerned. Includes bibliographical data regarding continuing publications and monographic studies in progress, as well as details of the operations of committees, training centers, regional meetings, etc. The information is given at some length, the catalogs averaging 150-odd large pages of text. Comprehensive index of names and subjects, with detailed breakdown under areas and broad subject fields." (Conover, p. 63)

United Nations, Office of Public Information. **Basic Facts About the United Nations.** 19th ed. New York: 1964, pp. 60. An outline of the structure and functions of the United Nations and the specialized agencies. Membership list included.

United Nations, Secretariat, Protocol and Liaison Section. **Delegations to the United Nations.** New York: 1946-. (See *Biographies: Personnel in Government, Diplomatic Corps, and International Organizations.*)

United Nations, Secretariat, Protocol and Liaison Section. **Permanent Missions to the United Nations.** New York: 1946–1955. (See *Biographies: Personnel in Government, Diplomatic Corps, and International Organizations.*)

United Nations, Secretary General. **Repertory of Practice of United Nations Organs.** 5 vols. with Supplements. New York: United Nations, 1955. It "constitutes a comprehensive summary of the decisions of United Nations organs, together with related material organized by charter articles, and presented in such a way as to throw light on questions of application and interpretation of the Charter which have arisen in practice. In five volumes, it covers all of the articles of the Charter in respect of which there have been decisions and discussions by the organs of the United Nations, for the period which they began functioning until 1 September 1954. Supplement No. 1 in two volumes continues the Repertory for the period 1 September 1954 to 31 August 1956." The supplements are not cumulative and thus should be read together with the Repertory itself. (Brimmer, p. 143)

UN Monthly Chronicle. New York: United Nations Office of Public Information, May 1964-. Published monthly except August. Its purpose is to advance understanding of the work of the United Nations. Comprehensive, documented accounts of U.N. activities and information on related agencies. Divided into several sections: Record of the Month, Pictures, Articles, and Documents. Supersedes *United Nations Review* (July 1954—April 1964) which, in turn, superseded United Nations Bulletin, an earlier publication of the same general intent.

United Nations:
Guides to Publications

Davis, Edward P. **Periodicals of International Organizations: Part I, The United Nations and Specialized Agencies; Part II, Inter-American Organizations.** Washington: Columbus Memorial Library, Pan American Union, 1950, pp. 21. (See *Periodicals: Guides to Periodicals.*)

Goodrich, Leland M., and Hambro, Edvard. **Charter of the United Nations: Commentary and Documents.** 2nd & rev. ed. Boston:

World Peace Foundation, 1949, pp. 710. "Select Bibliography, pp. 659–681. Lists official publications of the United Nations, generally and under its subdivisions; also publications of specialized and regional agencies, as well as unofficial documentary collections and books, pamphlets and articles concerning the United Nations." (Brown, p. 110)

International Labour Office, Library. **Bibliography on the International Labour Organization.** Geneva: 1954, pp. 68. This covers the period 1929–1953, continuing the *Bibliography of the International Labour Organization* published until 1929. It claims to be only a selected bibliography. In English and French. Has an alphabetical author index. "It includes: (1) earlier bibliographies on the I.L.O. and catalogues of its own publications, these being original sources which must necessarily be consulted to undertake a study of the work of the International Labour Organization; (2) reports and monographs prepared by the I.L.O., either to give a general view of its work, or to furnish substantial descriptions of its activity in a given period; (3) commercially published books, theses, official reports on the I.L.O., either of a general or special character or treating of the results of regular sessions of the International Labour Conference and of special and regional meetings organised by the I.L.O.; (4) a wide selection of periodical articles on the above subjects, insofar as they do more than simply summarise or reproduce information in I.L.O. publications." (Introduction, p. ii) This volume is Bibliographical Contribution No. 7, the bibliography being revised intermittently.

United Nations Educational, Scientific, and Cultural Organization. **International Social Science Bulletin.** Paris: 1941-. Quarterly. "A Review of Documents, Periodicals and Books fills the last forty or fifty pages of this journal devoted to social sciences in their relationships to international organizations. The first section lists and describes or abstracts documents and publications of the United Nations and the specialized agencies. The second part is an International Review of Periodicals, abstracting the chief contributions of the quarter having to do with U.N., and the last and shortest part reviews new books." (Conover, p. 64)

United Nations Headquarters Library. **Selected Bibliography of Specialized Agencies Related to the United Nations.** Bibliographical Series No. 1. New York: 1949, pp. 28. This was the first in a special subject bibliographical series issued by the U.N. Headquarters Library. These series are listed in the U.N. Publications Catalogue under the issuing bodies.

United Nations Library. **A Bibliography of the Charter of the United Nations.** New York: United Nations, 1955, pp. 128. "Extended bibliography on the Charter, including references to books, pamphlets, documents, and periodical material in many languages. This is one of the special subject bibliographies issued from time to time by the Headquarters Library of the United Nations." (Conover, p. 63)

United Nations Publications, 1945–1963: A Reference Catalogue. New York: United Nations, 1964, pp. v+72. A listing of all publications of the United Nations from its beginning. Only current editions of pamphlets from the Office of Public Information are listed. An annual publication of which *Ten Years of United Nations Publications: 1945–1955,* was the first cumulation, published 1955, and this volume is the second cumulation, superseding the annual volumes already published to date. Includes official records of General Assembly, Security Council, Trusteeship Council, Atomic Energy Commission, etc.

United Nations Publications in Microprint available at Readex Microprint Corporation, 115 University Place, New York 3, N.Y.: **United Nations Documents and Official Records, 1946-.**

United Nations:
Selected Documents and Records

Brimmer, Brenda. **A Guide to the Use of United Nations Documents, Including Reference to the Specialized Agencies and Special U.N. Bodies.** Dobbs Ferry, N.Y.: Oceana Publications, 1962, pp. xv+ 272. A description of the documentation system of the U.N., and including suggestions on techniques of research. Notice excellent bibliography on United Nations documentation on pp. 268–269.

Moor, Carol C., and Chamberlin, Waldo. **How to Use United Nations Documents.** New York: New York University Press, 1952, pp. 26.

"Manual explaining and listing the many tools and guides to the documents and publications of the United Nations—the check lists, information papers, and archives reference guides of the individual organs, the general *United Nations Documents Index,* special bibliographical studies. One chapter is given to a selected guide by subject —health, narcotic drugs, political, and so forth. Appendices list publications from the Department of Public Information, guides to the symbols system of U.N., and symbols used in press releases." (Conover, pp. 61–62)

United Nations. **Documents of the United Nations Conference on International Organization, San Francisco, 1945.** 22 vols. London and New York: United Nations Information Organizations, 1945–1955. Vol. I-. Historical background of the United Nations. Volume XV contains cumulative list of documents issued during the United Nations Conference in San Francisco. It also contains a list of documents issued by delegation chairmen. Volume XVI is index to Volumes I–XV. Volume XXI is a general index in English. Volume XXII is a general index in French. The index consists of two parts: the first is an index to the legislative history of the articles in the Charter and the second part contains an alphabetical index to the subject matter. (Brimmer, *passim*)

United Nations. **Treaty Series: Treaties and International Agreements Registered or Filed and Recorded with the Secretariat of the United Nations.** New York: United Nations, 1946-. (See *Treaty Collections.*)

United Nations Documents, 1941–1945. London and New York: Royal Institute of International Affairs, 1946, pp. 271. This collection of documents includes those concerning the origin of the U.N., its Charter, and other international organizations formed in association with it, to the end of 1945. In some cases, the preambles, appendices, lists of delegates or signatories, and other sections have been omitted.

United Nations Library. **United Nations Documents Index.** New York: United Nations, 1950-. Monthly. Index cumulated into bound volumes annually. Lists documents by agency, and is comprehensive current list of all documents and publications of the U.N. except for restricted material. This *Index* was preceded by *Checklist of United Nations Documents,* published 1949, covering the period 1946–1949, by the U.N. Library in Series F, with separate parts in one or more numbers, for each organ, e.g.: General Assembly, Security Council,

International Court of Justice, etc. For a guide to the use of these documents, see *How to Use United Nations Documents* by Carol Moor and Waldo Chamberlin (see above). The World Peace Foundation, Boston, also published 3 vols. ending in 1950, titled *Documents of International Organizations,* which was a quarterly bibliography of documents from the U.N. and other international organizations.

Watkins, James T., and Robinson, J. William. **General International Organization: A Source Book.** Princeton, N.J.: D. Van Nostrand Co., Inc., 1956, pp. xi+248. A volume of selected documents in three sections which include documents of the Nineteenth Century, documents related to the League of Nations, and documents related to the United Nations. In some cases whole documents are included; in other cases, excerpts.

Other

Council of Europe. **Handbook of European Organizations.** Strasbourg: Council of Europe, 1956, pp. viii+172. "The origins, aims and operation of the four principal international organizations in Europe (the Western European Union; the O.E.E.C.; the Council of Europe; and the European Coal and Steel Community) are stated in detail. Other European organizations are also covered. . . ." (Walford, p. 126)

Davis, Edward P. **Periodicals of International Organizations: Part I, The United Nations and Specialized Agencies; Part II, Inter-American Organizations.** Washington: Columbus Memorial Library, Pan American Union, 1950, pp. 21. (See *Periodicals: Guides to Periodicals.*)

European Year Book. The Hague: Nijhoff; London: Batsford, 1955-. Annual. "Published under the auspices of the Council of Europe. Text in English and French. Articles on aspects of European co-operation; text of documents of the O.E.E.C., Brussels Treaty Organization, etc. Includes list of publications of each organization, and a general annotated bibliography on European co-operation (including periodical articles)." (Walford, p. 95)

International Associations. Brussels: Union of International Associations, 1949-. Monthly. Supplements *Yearbook of International Organizations* and contains amendments to it. Also carries current news. Gives a full list of Forthcoming International Meetings as a regular feature, covering the following six months.

International Regional Organizations: Constitutional Foundations. Edited with introductory notes by Ruth C. Lawson. New York: Frederick A. Praeger, Inc., 1962, pp. xviii+387. Collection of basic documents of all international organizations of a regional character founded since World War II, e.g., NATO, Council of Europe, European Coal and Steel Community, European Economic Community, Arab League, Warsaw Pact, Organization of American States, etc.

International Scientific Organizations: A Guide to Their Library, Documentation, and Information Services. Prepared under the Direction of Kathrine O. Murra. Washington, D.C.: Library of Congress, 1962, pp. xi+794. Compiled and published under a grant from the National Science Foundation as one of its International Science Information Studies. Information was compiled from questionnaires, and 449 organizations are included in the volume. Science was "interpreted broadly" to include technology, agriculture, and medicine. Reports are listed alphabetically, in English, with French or Spanish usually used as second language for name.

League of Nations. **Handbook of International Organizations.** Geneva: 1939, pp. 491. Purpose of publication was to provide a source of information on international organizations. The organizations are classified according to the subjects with which they deal. The organizations of the League itself are not included, nor are those international organizations operated solely for profit, nor those whose existence is on a purely national basis. Gives such data as headquarters, foundation, object, members, governing body, officers, activities, official publications.

Leonard, Leonard Larry. **International Organization.** 1st ed. New York: McGraw-Hill, 1951, pp. 630. ". . . institutions have been selected which play a more significant role in world affairs, reveal the breadth of problems governments have sought to resolve through international organizations, and display variations in their structures and procedures. In addition to the genealogy of such organizations and the circumstances attending their birth, this volume will examine the processes of international organizations—'what makes them run.'

The focus for this examination is the practice of governments as they relate to international organizations." (Preface, p. viii)

Peaslee, Amos Jenkins. **International Governmental Organizations: Constitutional Documents.** 2 vols., 2nd ed., revised. The Hague: Nijhoff, 1961. Documents in this work relate only to international organizations of a governmental nature themselves and that have been created by governments. Vol. I begins with a general summary and separate tabulations of the types of documents from which these organizations derive their authority, the origin of the organizations with dates of their present constitutional documents, their functions, methods of financial support, relationships with other international governmental organizations, and their headquarters by city and country. This chapter is followed by a chapter on the details of each organization. The document from which each derives its authority is fully reproduced, and in many instances, a bibliography is appended. Vol. II contains a general index.

Robertson, A. H. **European Institutions: Co-operation, Integration, Unification.** Published under the auspices of the London Institute of World Affairs. New York: Frederick A. Praeger, Inc., 1959, pp. xix+372. This volume describes the structure and function of seven European institutions: OEEC, Council of Europe, NATO, Western European Union, the Coal and Steel Community, the Economic Community, and Euratom, with information about their principal activities. Eight smaller organizations are described briefly.

Union des Associations Internationales. **Les Congrès Internationaux de 1681 à 1899: List Complete.** Brussels: 1960, pp. 76. A chronological list of the first approximately 2,000 (of 20,000) international congresses, giving dates and places. There is a subject index in French and English. The text is in French.

Union of International Associations. **Directory of Periodicals Published by International Organizations.** 2nd ed. Brussels: 1959, pp. x+241. (See *Periodicals: Guides to Periodicals.*)

Union of International Associations. **International Institutions and International Organizations: A Select Bibliography.** Compiled by G. P. Speekaert. Brussels: U.I.A., 1956, pp. 116. "Lists 783 numbered publications in 9 groups (including 8. Yearbooks and directories; 9. Periodicals). Includes material on the League of Nations, International Labour Organization, the United Nations (and its Specialized Agencies), the European Coal and Steel Community, etc. No annotations." (Walford, p. 50)

Union of International Associations. **Yearbook of International Organizations.** Brussels: U.I.A., 1948-. Irregular, 1962–63 edition available. Alternate English and French editors. "Broadly classified; for each organization gives address, status, history, purposes, types of membership, structure, officers, finance, activities, and publications. Indexes of key-words in titles, abbreviations of titles, and places. Includes both governmental and non-governmental organizations. Valuable for its full detail." (Walford, p. 51)

United Nations Educational, Scientific, and Cultural Organization. **Directory of International Scientific Organizations.** 2nd ed. Paris: UNESCO, 1953, pp. 312. "This edition lists 264 organizations, arranged alphabetically within sections covering the basic sciences, agriculture, engineering, medicine, and miscellaneous subjects. Details given include official name and its abbreviation, address, nature (governmental or otherwise), aims, governing body and officers, members, commissions, facilities, finances, meetings, voting, publications, relations with other international organizations, short history, bibliographical references, comments." (Walford, p. 201)

UNESCO, Social Science Clearing House. **International Organizations in the Social Sciences: A Summary Description of the Structure and Activities of Non-Governmental Organizations in Consultative Relationship with Unesco and Specialized in the Social Sciences.** Rev. & augmented ed. Paris: UNESCO, 1961, pp. 145. Deals with 18 selected bodies from among those which are recognized international, non-governmental organizations which devote their activities to the social sciences and have been approved for consultative relationships with UNESCO. For each of the 18 organizations the book gives: aims, activities, officers and committees, record of conferences (from the organization's beginning to date of publication), and constitution.

U.S. Citizens in World Affairs: **A Directory of Non-Governmental Organizations.** Compiled by Katherine C. Garrigue. New York: Foreign Policy Association, Inc., 1953, pp. iii+389. A directory of nongovernmental organizations in the U.S., concerned wholly or in part with the field of international relations. Listed are 434 organizations. Organizations excluded from the list were those of an official nature, those connected with academic institutions, societies devoted exclusively to cultural or social research, and regional and local groups except the Council on World Affairs.

U. S. Department of State, Bureau of United Nations Affairs. **Inter-**

national Organizations in which the United States Participates, 1949. Washington, D.C.: U.S. Government Printing Office, 1950, pp. viii+ 335. This is the first revision of *International Agencies in which the United States Participates,* issued in 1946. The present volume includes information to June 30, 1949. Both volumes present basic data related to origin and development of the organization; membership; purposes, powers, and functions; finances; structure; United States relations, etc.

Watkins, James T., and Robinson, J. William. **General International Organization: A Source Book.** Princeton, N.J.: D. Van Nostrand Co., Inc., 1956, pp. xi+248. (See *International Organizations: United Nations, Selected Documents and Records.*)

Interviews and Oral Histories

Columbia University, Oral History Research Office. **The Oral History Collection of Columbia University.** New York: 1964, pp. 181. Lists the oral history memoirs which are deposited in Special Collections, Butler Library, Columbia University, as well as those in process. "This volume, complete to February 1, 1964, supplants our 1960 edition, its 1962 supplement, and the listing printed in our Fifteenth Anniversary Report. It describes memoirs totaling 200,401 pages, not counting those in process. Approximately 60 per cent of the Collection (118,598 pages) may be read at this time." (Introduction, p. 13) Students of International Relations should take special note of the sections on Special Projects and Lectures, Seminars and Forums. Special Reports includes Chinese History Project, Eisenhower Administration, Flying Tigers, Dag Hammarskjold as Secretary General, Kennedy Administration, Marshall Plan, Occupation of Japan, Psychoanalytic Movement. Lectures, Seminars and Forums among other topics includes American Foreign Policy (a panel discussion); a lecture on Man and Nuclear Energy; and a group discussion on United Nations Conference, San Francisco, by distinguished scholars.

Ryan, Milo. **History in Sound: A Descriptive Listing of the KIRO-CBS Collection of Broadcasts of the World War II Years and After, in the Phonoarchive of the University of Washington.** Seattle: University of Washington Press, 1963, pp. xxv+617. The collection covers the time period from Hitler's speech to the Reichstag on January 30, 1939, to the October 22, 1962, address by President Kennedy during the Cuban crisis. Notice particularly the section on Talks and Interviews. It includes 22 speeches by Winston Churchill, 6 by Hitler, 18 by Kennedy, etc.

Newspapers

This section is divided into two parts. The first, Directories (Worldwide), gives statistical information concerning newspapers in the United States and foreign countries, and, in one case, some evaluation of foreign papers. In the second category only indexes to newspaper articles in the English language are included.

Directories (Worldwide)

American Newspapers 1821–1936: A Union List of Files Available in the United States and Canada. Edited by Winifred Gregory. New York: H. W. Wilson Co., 1937, pp. 791. Edited under the auspices of the Bibliographical Society of America. A listing of depositories of files of newspapers for the dates given in libraries both in the U.S. and Canada, as well as newspaper offices, county courthouses, and private collections. Organs of religious denominations, labor unions, and fraternal lodges have been omitted. Arrangement is alphabetical by state or province and city. The work also contains a bibliography of union lists of newspapers, listed by country, as well as notes on newspapers published in foreign countries found in the libraries of the U.S. and Canada and a list of other special collections.

Editor & Publisher International Yearbook. New York: Editor & Publisher Co., Inc., 1921-. Complete list of all daily papers in the U.S. and Canada and their circulation, with names of executive personnel. Also contains the names of daily newspapers in every country, with circulation, language in which printed, and, although not uniformly, in many instances, names of the editor and publisher.

Merrill, John C., *et al.* **The Foreign Press.** Baton Rouge: Louisiana

State University Press, 1964, pp. xi+256. A revised edition of John C. Merrill, *A Handbook of the Foreign Press*. Described by author as a "basic survey textbook." Deals principally with newspapers and magazines. Intended primarily for journalism students, it includes some comments on the appeal in terms of political opinion of major newspapers in Western Europe, the U.S.S.R. and other Communist countries, the Middle East, Southeast Asia, the Far East, Latin America, Australia, Canada, and Africa, and some comments on the position of the press in each country, and economic and political factors which influence it. Helpful if one wishes to make some general evaluation of a foreign news source.

Newspapers on Microfilm. 5th ed. Compiled under direction of George A. Schwegmann, Jr. Washington: 1963, pp. xv+305. ". . . Includes all of the information concerning microfilmed newspapers that had come to the attention of the Microfilming Clearing House of the Library of Congress prior to June 1, 1963. It contains approximately 16,000 entries, representing about 4,000 foreign newspapers and more than 12,000 domestic newspapers. . . . In this edition, as in the third and fourth editions, an effort has been made to show the location of positive copies as well [as negative]." (Preface, p. iii)

Newspapers and Periodicals [N. W. Ayer and Son's Directory]. Philadelphia: N. W. Ayer & Son, Inc., 1880-. Maps, annual. Title varies 1880–1930. "Useful gazetteer information; gives date of foundation, frequency, price, size, circulation, name of editor, and address. Rather confusing arrangement in a dozen separate sections, with index of periodical titles (but not of newspapers)." (Walford, p. 46)

U.S. House of Representatives, Committee on Un-American Activities. **Guide to Subversive Organizations and Publications (and Appendixes) Revised and Published December 1, 1961 to Supersede Guide Published on January 2, 1957 (Including Index).** Washington, D.C.: U.S. Government Printing Office, 1961, pp. 248+index, xxxviii. Part I consists of an alphabetical listing of "Organizations cited as Communist or Communist-Front by Federal Authorities" with excerpts from the citation and the source of the citation included. Part II lists "Publications cited as Communist or Communist-Front by Federal Authorities." Parts III and IV are listings of organizations and publications, respectively, "Cited as Communist or Communist-Front by State or Territorial Investigating Committees." Most of these publications are newspapers.

Willing's Press Guide. London: James Willing, Limited, 1894-. A guide and advertisers' directory and handbook. Title varies; after 1927, it is known as *Willing's Press Guide.* Covers press of the U.K. and Commonwealth and foreign publications. Includes trade and special interest journals. Lists times of publication, price, publisher, and address.

Indexes to Articles

The Christian Science Monitor Index. Corvallis, Oregon: Helen M. Cropsey, 1960-. Monthly with semi-annual and annual cumulations. The *Cumulated 1960 Annual* indexed the Western and New England editions; the *Cumulated 1961 Annual* indexed the Eastern, Western, and New England editions; and the *Cumulated 1962 Annual* indexed Eastern, Western, and Midwestern editions. "The edition pattern is now set with these three editions which cover the Western Hemisphere." (Preface)

The Current Digest of the Soviet Press: Consisting of Translations from Soviet Periodicals with Bibliographical Index of Soviet Newspapers. New York: Joint Committee on Slavic Studies, 1949-. "Weekly. Complete indexing of articles in *Izvestia* and *Pravda,* and partial indexing of 40 other periodicals. The more important articles are either abstracted or given complete translations." (Walford, p. 54)

The New York Times Index. New York: New York Times, 1913-. Beginning January 1930, the *Index* became a monthly publication with quarterly and annual cumulations, where it previously had been a quarterly volume only. The annual volume from 1930 indexed all the news, special features, etc., printed in daily and Sunday editions of the *Times* during the year. Since 1948 the publication has been semimonthly with annual cumulations. Arrangement is alphabetical. Entries are under names and subjects, and cross-references to persons and related events are given in addition to the date, page, and column. There are also brief abstracts compiled chronologically and arranged alphabetically under subject headings, followed by date, page, and column references to the original article.

The Times (London). **Index to The Times.** London: *The Times,* 1906-. "1906–1913 published as *The Annual Index to 'The Times';* 1914– Jan./Feb. 1957 as *The Official Index to 'The Times.'* Monthly with annual cumulations 1906 to June 1914; quarterly, July 1914–1956; bi-monthly, 1957-. Reference to date, page, and column; indexes the latest edition of each day, but includes also items printed only in earlier editions. Supplements issued with the paper are included (e.g., *Times Literary Supplement* 1906–21)." (Walford, p. 54)

The Times (London). **Palmer's Index to The Times Newspaper.** Wiltshire, England, etc.: S. Palmer, 1868–1943. Title and place of publication have varied. "Quarterly volumes cover 1790 to June 1941. Briefer entries and less accurate indexing than the *Official Index,* but valuable because it goes back almost to the beginning of *The Times.* Deaths are grouped under that heading, with no references in the body of the index." (Walford, p. 54)

The Wall Street Journal Index. New York: Dow Jones & Co., 1958-. The Index is compiled from the *final Eastern edition;* thus, paging and content may vary in those editions published in other cities. The annual index is divided into three sections: Corporate News, General News, and the Dow Jones closing averages for each day of the year.

Periodicals

Indexes to Periodical Articles

The Current Digest of the Soviet Press: Consisting of Translations from Soviet Periodicals with Bibliographical Index of Soviet Newspapers. New York: Joint Committee on Slavic Studies, 1949-. (See *Newspapers: Indexes to Articles.*)

Current Thought on Peace and War: A Semi-Annual Digest of Literature and Research in Progress on the Problems of World Order and Conflict. Durham, N.C., 1960-. (See *Abstracts.*)

Fondation Nationale des Sciences Politiques. **Bulletin Analytique de Documentation Politique, Économique et Sociale Contemporaine.** Paris: Presses Universitaires de France, 1946-. Bimonthly "Classified list of periodical articles selected from leading economic and political journals of the world, with brief annotations or abstracts. The plan of classification is printed on the back cover of each number, and there is an annual index. The classification is first by general studies and theories (political sciences, economic sciences, economic situation, agrarian questions, history of economic doctrines, social sciences, etc.), then by national problems, with country division, and last, international relations. The publication receives support from the official Centre National de la Recherche Scientifique. In its compilation over 800 periodicals are examined, most of the material abstracted being current within three or four months." (Conover, p. 14)

Historical Abstracts, 1775–1945: A Quarterly of Abstracts of Historical Articles Appearing Currently in Periodicals the World Over. Edited by Erich H. Boehm. Santa Barbara, Calif.: Clio Press, 1955-. (See *Abstracts.*)

Index to Labor Union Periodicals: A Cumulative Subject Index to Materials from a Selected List of Newspapers and Journals Published by Major Labor Unions. Ann Arbor: Bureau of Industrial

Relations, University of Michigan, 1960-. Published monthly. Cumulated annually and semiannually. It provides a subject index with brief descriptions of material in approximately 41 labor union periodicals.

Index Medicus. Washington, D.C.: National Library of Medicine, 1960-. Approximately 1,500 journals are indexed by subject and by author. Monthly.

Index to Periodical Articles Related to Law: Selected from Journals not Included in the Index to Legal Periodicals. Hackensack, N.J.: Fred B. Rothman & Co., Law Library Service, 1958-. Bimonthly.

International Index to Periodicals: A Guide to Periodical Literature in the Social Sciences and Humanities. New York: H. W. Wilson Co., 1913-. First published as *Readers' Guide Supplement,* to provide indexing for special periodicals. Scholarly periodicals and publications of learned societies were first included in the *Supplement* in 1919. The third volume of the permanent cumulations, published 1924, was titled *International Index to Periodicals,* because the material indexed had become international in scope. In 1962 the subtitle, *A Guide to Periodical Literature in the Social Sciences and Humanities,* was added. Listed are the periodicals indexed (approximately 180 publications in the 1962 permanent volume), their abbreviations, and a key. There is both an author and a subject index. Current issues are published four times annually; these are cumulated into annual volumes, which are, in turn, cumulated into permanent volumes. (These have been cumulated approximately every 3 years since 1928; prior to that the period of permanent cumulation varied.)

Internationale Bibliographie der Zeitschriftenliteratur. Osnabrück: Dietrich, 1897-. "The most extensive of periodical indexes. Known as 'IBZ' and 'Dietrich.' Originally published in Leipzig. [In 3 parts, published separately:]

"Abt. A: **Bibliographie der deutschen Zeitschriftenliteratur, mit Einschluss von Sammelwerken.** 1897-. An alphabetical subject index. Semi-annual . . . with no cumulations; six-monthly author index; now indexes about 3,600 German-language periodicals and 45 newspapers. The main work starts in 1896, but supplementary volumes carry it back to 1861.

"Abt. B: **Bibliographie der Fremdsprachigen Zeitschriftenliteratur. Repertoire Bibliographique International des Revues. International Index to Periodicals.** 1911–1919, 1925-. Frequency varies in early years; now semi-annual with no cumulations; six-monthly author index. 1920–1924 not published. 1943/44–1948/49 not yet published. An alphabetical subject index to periodicals in non-German languages 1911–1919; subject and author indexes 1925 to date. Now covers about 3,200 titles from 30 countries and in 20 languages. In spite of heavy abbreviation and closely-set text, *Dietrich* is the best general index in that its coverage is the fullest, especially for countries not covered adequately by indexes of their own; pt. B is of great value to non-German libraries.

"Abt. C: **Bibliographie der Rezensionen und Referate.** v. 1–77: 1940–1943. The 1900–1911 v. only indexed German reviews; the 1912–1943 v. were published in two series, numbered alternately, one indexing book reviews in German periodicals and the other non-German. The same coverage as pts. A & B respectively." (Walford, p. 47)

Population Index. Princeton, N.J.: Office of Population Research, Princeton University, and Population Association of America, 1935-. "Index and abstracts of demographic literature, classified according to broad aspects—general studies and theory, regional studies, spatial distribution, mortality, etc., with specific subdivisions. A section on official statistics is broken down by country. References are to books, pamphlets, documents and periodical literature. There are included a geographical index, an author index, and tables of vital statistics." (Conover, p. 57) Quarterly.

Public Affairs Information Service. **Bulletin of the Public Affairs Information Service, Annual Cumulations.** New York: Public Affairs Information Service, 1915-. The P.A.I.S. publishes weekly bulletins, which list alphabetically by subject current books, government documents, periodical articles, pamphlets, etc. in the field of public affairs and economics. Publications from all English-speaking countries are included; emphasis is on factual and statistical information. Cumulated bulletins are published five times a year and the fifth cumulated issue becomes a cumulated permanent annual volume. Listed at the beginning of the annual volume are a key to periodical references, a directory of publishers and organizations, and a list of publications analyzed.

Readers' Guide to Periodical Literature. Vol. I-, 1900-. [New York:] H. W. Wilson Co., 1905-. Lists periodicals in varying numbers with each volume. Included are scientific and scholarly publications, but general periodicals are also included. Articles are usually indexed under author, subject, and title. Indexing is cumulative and includes permanent cumulated volumes, supplemental annual volumes (which are cumulated into permanent volumes every two years), and semimonthly issues, which are cumulated into the annual volumes, thus giving almost current information.

U.S. Library of Congress. **Monthly List of Russian Accessions.** Washington, D.C.: U.S. Government Printing Office, 1948-. A record of publications in the Russian language received by the Library of Congress. The *Lists* are divided into two parts: The first covers monographic literature (from 1945); the second lists the contents of Russian periodicals (from 1947). Material is classified by subject, arranged alphabetically. Some of the subjects covered are General and Reference Works, Bibliography, Education, Political Science, Science, Social Sciences, Law, History, and Economic History. Microfilm copies or photostatic copies of the listed items which are in the Library of Congress may be ordered.

Recherches: Bulletin d'Information Bibliographique et Documentaire. [Research: Bibliographical and Documentary Information Bulletin]. Strasbourg: Bibliothèque du Conseil de l'Europe, 1951-. Bimonthly. "Bibliographical publication compiled from material received in the Documentation Centre of the Council of Europe and adapted to the use of the Secretariat-General and members. The body of the bulletin is a selected listing of articles from current periodicals and newspapers of Western Europe and the United States, in classified arrangement under three main divisions, organizations of Europe, international organizations, and national and world problems. This is followed by a list of new books and documents acquired by the Library. A number of issues have contained as appendix a separate pamphlet, between 40 and 50 pages long, bibliography on a special subject. . . . " (Conover, p. 71)

U.S. Dept. of State, Library. **International Politics: A Selective Monthly.** Washington, D.C.: 1956-. "New list being prepared by the Department of State Library on the basis of items examined during the month. Entries are chiefly for unofficial material, most of it in English—monographs and articles found in a selected list of periodicals which are analyzed regularly in the Library." The bibliography primarily for circulation within the Department, but copies to be distributed to limited number of libraries and institutions. (Conover, p. 23)

U.S. Library of Congress, Processing Dept. **East European Acces-**

sions List. Washington, D.C.: U.S. Government Printing Office, Sept./Oct. 1951-. Monthly. "Comprehensive catalog of publications currently received by the Library of Congress and other cooperating American libraries. There are included monographic works and periodical contributions printed in ten countries of East Europe or elsewhere in the languages of these countries: Albania, Bulgaria, Czechoslovakia, Estonia, Hungary, Latvia, Lithuania, Poland, Rumania, Yugoslavia." The list is followed by a detailed subject index. (Conover, pp. 85–86)

Guides to Periodicals

Andriot, John L. **Guide to U.S. Government Serials & Periodicals.** McLean, Virginia: Documents Index, 1962-. Vol. I lists current serials and periodicals of the Washington, D.C. area agencies. Vol. II contains lists of "releases and other ephemeral material." Vol. III, which has not appeared as of September 1964, will list all publications of agencies outside the Washington area. Availability of publications, prices for periodicals, with some description of publication, usually taken from publication itself. There is no background information about the agencies themselves, but a separate volume is planned for the future which will provide this information.

British Union-Catalogue of Periodicals: A Record of the Periodicals of the World, from the Seventeenth Century to the Present Day in British Libraries. Edited by J. D. Stewart, with M. E. Hammond and E. Saenger. 4 vols. London: Butterworth Scientific Publications, 1955–1958. "The fullest list of periodicals ever published, with more than 140,000 titles permanently filed in 441 libraries in the United Kingdom. Covers a wide field, including annuals, but excludes newspapers after 1799, directories and timetables, and some ephemera; the National Central Library holds records of some entries excluded (e.g., timetables and annual reports). Includes complete holdings of many general libraries, with specialized material from special libraries and selected items from a great many other sources; this policy of partial coverage causes much unevenness in reports of holdings. Arrangement is by earliest title (or earliest form of name of society), with liberal references; gives changes of title, volume numbering and dates, and notes existence (but not locations) of cumulated indexes." (Walford, p. 39)

Davis, Edward P. **Periodicals of International Organizations: Part I, The United Nations and Specialized Agencies; Part II, Inter-American Organizations.** Washington, D.C.: Columbus Memorial Library, Pan American Union, 1950, pp. 21. " . . . a selection has been made of what the author considers to be the more important periodicals of the major organizations of an inter-governmental character." (p. 1) These periodicals of international organizations are divided into three main categories: (1) world-wide organizations; (2) regional organizations; (3) the postwar transitional bodies. Both Part I and Part II have a section called A Classified Bibliography.

Farber, Evan Ira. **Classified List of Periodicals for the College Library.** 4th ed. Boston: The F. W. Faxon Company, Inc., 1957, pp. xi+146. A list of periodicals with brief notes giving title, place of publication, date first published, and some brief description of each.

Historical Periodicals: An Annotated World List of Historical and Related Serial Publications. Edited by Eric H. Boehm and Lalit Adolphus. Santa Barbara, Calif., and Munich, Germany: Clio Press, 1961, pp. xix+619. This volume includes a list of current periodicals. Those which discontinued publication on or after 1957 are included with a note as to the year of termination. It is an annotated directory of serial publications containing articles on historical topics. This is intended as an all-inclusive, rather than an evaluative listing. Approximately 5,000 periodicals are listed.

Index to Foreign Legal Periodicals. London: Institute of Advanced Legal Studies, University of London in cooperation with the American Association of Law Libraries, 1960-. Quarterly with annual cumulations. It indexes "the main legal periodicals dealing with international law (public and private), comparative law and the municipal law of all countries of the world other than the United States, the British Isles and the countries of the British Commonwealth. . . . " (Preface)

Index to Legal Periodicals. New York: H. W. Wilson Co., 1908-. Monthly from October to August. Annual and 3-year cumulations. Published for the American Association of Law Libraries. The cumulated volumes contain an author index, subject index, table of cases, and also, beginning in 1940, a book review index.

International Committee of Comparative Law. **Catalogue des Sources**

de Documentation Juridique dans le Monde [A Register of Legal Documentation in the World]. Paris: UNESCO, 1953, pp. 362. (See *International Law*.)

Ulrich's Periodicals Directory: A Classified Guide to a Selected List of Current Periodicals, Foreign and Domestic. 10th ed. Edited by E. C. Graves. New York: R. R. Bowker Co., 1963, pp. 667. Lists several thousand titles, "giving date of foundation, frequency, price, size and address. Indicates features of each periodical, such as illustrations, book reviews, and bibliographies, and shows by which of the major abstracting and indexing services it is covered, if any. Classified arrangement, with title index. The only large-scale, select list, and an invaluable tool. Omits annual reviews." (Walford, p. 41)

Union of International Associations. **Directory of Periodicals Published by International Organizations.** 2nd ed. Brussels: 1959, pp. x+241. Published with the assistance of UNESCO. Supersedes 1st edition, with same title, published in 1953. Lists periodical publications of supranational and intergovernmental institutions, periodical publications of international nongovernmental organizations. There is also an index with organizations in English and French, the titles of periodicals in their different editions, and a geographical index. About 1,300 periodicals are listed.

Union List of Serials in Libraries of the United States and Canada. 2nd ed. Edited by W. Gregory. New York: H. W. Wilson Co., 1943, pp. 3065. Supplements: 1941–43 (1945, pp. 1123); 1944–49 (1953, pp. 1365); 1950–52 not published. "Lists more than 120,000 titles in about 650 libraries. Gives bibliographical details as well as holdings. Excludes foreign newspapers after 1820, and all American newspapers, as well as certain minor and ephemeral types of periodical. Covers more libraries but fewer titles than [British Union-Catalogue of Periodicals], and includes roughly the same classes of serial. A useful 'Bibliography of Union Lists of Serials,' listing 359 items, is on pp. 3053–65." *New Serial Titles* (1953–) is the official continuation of the *Union List of Serials*. (Walford, p. 41)

United Nations Educational, Scientific, and Cultural Organization. **Liste Mondiale des Periodiques Specialises dans les Sciences Sociales.** [World List of Social Science Periodicals.] Paris: 1953, pp. 161. "Reference guide prepared as part of the program of Unesco and the Co-ordinating Committee on Documentation in the Social Sciences (now International Committee for Social Sciences

Documentation) . . . Arranged by country of publication, the list contains titles of about 600 specialized periodicals published in over fifty countries—'solely those of a scientific character, i.e., those regularly publishing original studies and articles by university specialists or other experts in the various branches of these sciences.' Each periodical is explained fully, data including French and English translations of titles in other languages, publisher, editors, frequency, year of foundation, average size, and a content description of a typical issue. Four indexes list titles, scientific institutions publishing periodicals, specific subjects, and disciplines. Fields covered are social sciences in general, sociocultural sciences, economics, political sciences, statistics. The journals listed were appearing in 1951." (Conover, p. 23)

U.S. Library of Congress, Africana Section. **Serials for African Studies.** Compiled by Helen F. Conover. Washington, D.C.: 1961, pp. 163. A listing of all periodicals and other publications which regularly publish information about Africa. About 2,000 serials, some annotations.

U.S. Library of Congress. **New Serial Titles: A Union List of Serials Commencing Publication after December 31, 1949.** Washington, D.C.: 1953- Replaces *Serial Titles Newly Received* (1951–1952), which was limited to Library of Congress holdings. Beginning in November 1955 *New Serial Titles* has also been published as *New Serial Titles: Classified Subject Arrangement. New Serial Titles* "lists periodicals received in the Library of Congress and other major U.S. Libraries (203 in 1955). The 1955 volume contains 35,500 entries, limited to serials with title pages using the Roman alphabet, and to serials with Cyrillic, Greek, Gaelic, and Hebraic title pages (regardless of the alphabet or language of the text); excludes newspapers. The annual volume gives place of publication, dates, class and location; frequency, address, and subscription price are given in the monthly issues only. Valuable as the fullest listing of new titles published anywhere. Is the official continuation of Gregory's *Union List of Serials* for titles published from 1950 onwards. Annual volumes will be cumulated 5-yearly (1950–55, 1956–60), then 10-yearly. From 1955 a new section (Changes in Serials) lists title changes, suspensions, cessations, etc. It is intended to include Oriental languages." (Walford, p. 41)

Zimmerman, Irene. **A Guide to Current Latin American Periodicals: Humanities and Social Sciences.** Gainesville, Florida: Kallman Publishing Co., 1961, pp. x+357. Intended as an annotated, evaluative bibliography, the basic listing is by country, with titles accompanied by annotations in this section. There is also included a subject listing and a chronological listing. Periodicals are defined for purposes of this book as publications which appear in numbered sequence, not more frequently than once a week, are independent of other publications, and whose contents are nonmonographic.

Selected Journals Pertinent to International Relations

The American Behavioral Scientist. Princeton, N.J.: 1957-. Monthly except July and August.

American Economic Review. Evanston, Illinois: 1911-. 5 times a year. Organ of the American Economic Association.

American Historical Review. New York: 1895-. Quarterly. Official journal of the American Historical Association.

American Journal of Economics and Sociology. New York: 1941-. Quarterly.

The American Journal of International Law. Washington, D.C.: American Society of International Law, 1907-. With Supplements. Quarterly.

The American Political Science Review. Washington, D.C.: American Political Science Association, 1906-. Quarterly.

The Annals of the American Academy of Political and Social Science. Philadelphia: 1890-. Bimonthly.

Aussenpolitik. Stuttgart: Deutsches Verlags-Anstalt, May 1950-. Monthly.

Background: Journal of the International Studies Association. San Francisco, Calif.: Institute for Research on International Behavior, San Francisco State College, 1957-. Quarterly.

Bulletin of the Atomic Scientists: A Journal of Science and Public Affairs. Chicago: Education Foundation for Nuclear Science, Inc., 1945-. Monthly—September to June.

The Canadian Journal of Economics and Political Science. Toronto, Canada: University of Toronto Press, 1935-. Quarterly.

Chronique de Politique Étrangère. Brussels: Institut des Relations Internationales, 1948-. Bimonthly.

Current History. Philadelphia: Events Publishing Co., 1914-. Monthly.

Diplomatist: The Review of the Diplomatic and Consular World. London: Diplomatist Publications Ltd., 1947-. Monthly.

Documentary Material on Social Problems. Strasbourg: Documentation and Library Section, Council of Europe, 1956-. Quarterly.

France, Direction de la Documentation. **La Documentation Française** (several series). Paris: 1944-. Quarterly.

The Economist. London: 1943-. Weekly.

Europa-Archiv. Frankfurt am Main: 1946-. Bimonthly.

Foreign Affairs: An American Quarterly Review. New York: Council on Foreign Relations, 1922-.

Foreign Service Journal. Washington, D.C.: American Foreign Service Association, 1924-. Monthly.

India Quarterly: A Journal of International Affairs. New Delhi: Published by Asia Publishing House for Indian Council of World Affairs, 1945-.

International Affairs. London: The Royal Institute of International Affairs, 1922-. Quarterly.

International Affairs: A Monthly Journal of Political Analysis. Moscow, 1955-.

The International and Comparative Law Quarterly. London: British Institute of International and Comparative Law, 1952-.

International Conciliation. New York: Carnegie Endowment for International Peace, 1907-. Frequency varies. Since 1955, 5 times a year.

International Journal. Toronto: Canadian Institute of International Affairs, 1946-. Quarterly.

International Labour Review. Geneva: International Labour Office, 1921-. Monthly. Issued in English, French, and Spanish editions.

International Relations Digest of Periodical Literature. Berkeley: University of California, Bureau of International Relations, 1950-. Monthly.

International Review of Administrative Science. Brussels: International Institute of Administrative Sciences, 1928-. Quarterly.

International Social Science Journal. Paris: UNESCO, 1949-. Quarterly.

The Journal of Asian Studies. Ann Arbor, Michigan: The Association for Asian Studies, Inc., 1941-. Quarterly.

The Journal of Conflict Resolution: A Quarterly for Research Related to War and Peace. Ann Arbor, Michigan: The Center for Research on Conflict Resolution, University of Michigan, 1957-. Quarterly.

Journal of International Affairs. New York: 1947-. Semiannually.

Journal of Modern History. Chicago: University of Chicago Press, 1929-. Quarterly.

The Journal of Political Economy. Chicago: The University of Chicago Press, 1892-. Quarterly.

The Journal of Politics. Gainesville, Florida: Southern Political Science Association, University of Florida, 1939-. Quarterly.

Journal of Social Issues. Ann Arbor, Michigan: Society for Psychological Study of Social Issues, Institute for Social Research, University of Michigan, 1945-. Quarterly.

Journal of the Science of Food and Agriculture. London: Society of Chemical Industry, 1950-. Monthly.

Midwest Journal of Political Science. Detroit: Wayne State University Press, 1957-. Quarterly.

Military Affairs. Washington, D.C.: American Military Institute, 1937-. Quarterly.

Orbis: A Quarterly Journal of World Affairs. Philadelphia: Foreign Policy Research Institute, University of Pennsylvania, 1957-.

Pacific Affairs. New York: Institute of Pacific Relations, 1926-. Quarterly.

Political Affairs. New York: New Century Publishers, 1922-. Monthly.

The Political Quarterly. London: Stevens & Sons, 1930-.

Political Science Quarterly. New York: Academy of Political Science, Columbia University, 1886-.

Politique Étrangère. Paris: Centre d'Études de Politique Étrangère, 1936-. Bimonthly.

U.S. Information Agency. **Problems of Communism.** Washington, D.C.: U.S. Government Printing Office, 1952-. Bimonthly.

Public Administration Review. Chicago: American Society for Public Administration, 1940-. Quarterly.

Public Finance: International Quarterly Journal Devoted to the Study of Fiscal Policy and Related Problems. Haarlem, The Netherlands: 1946-.

The Public Opinion Quarterly. Princeton, N.J.: Princeton University Press, 1937-.

The Quarterly Journal of Economics. Cambridge, Mass.: Harvard University Press, 1886-.

The Review of Politics. Notre Dame, Indiana: University of Notre Dame, 1939-. Quarterly.

Revista de Economía Política. Madrid: 1945-. Quarterly (irregular).

Revista de Estudios Políticos. Madrid: Instituto de Estudios Políticos, 1941-. Bimonthly.

Revue de l'Institut de Sociologie. Brussels: Université Libre, Institut de Sociologie Solvay, 1920-. Quarterly.

Revue du Droit Public et de la Science Politique en France et à l'Étranger. Paris: Librairie Générale de Droit et de Jurisprudence, 1894-. Quarterly.

Revue Française de Science Politique. Paris: 1951-. Quarterly.

Revue Historique. Paris: Presses Universitaires de France, 1876-. Quarterly.

Revue Internationale des Sciences Administratives. Brussels: l'Institut International des Sciences Administratives, 1928-. Quarterly.

Revue Politique et Parlementaire. Paris, 1894-. Monthly.

Rivista Internazionale di Scienze Sociali. Milano: Università Cattolica del Sacro Cuore, 1893-. Bimonthly.

Slavic Review: American Quarterly of Soviet and East European Studies. Menasha, Wisconsin: G. Banta Publishing Co., 1945-.

The Slavonic and East European Review. Menasha, Wisconsin: G. Banta Publishing Co., 1922-. Frequency varies.

Soviet Studies. Edited at the University of Glasgow. Oxford: Basil Blackwell, 1949-. Quarterly.

UNESCO Courier. New York: 1948-. Monthly. (See *International Organizations: United Nations, Activities and General Information.*)

The Western Political Quarterly. Salt Lake City, Utah: Institute of Government, University of Utah, 1948-.

World Affairs Interpreter. Los Angeles: University of Southern California, 1930-. Quarterly.

World Federalist. The Hague: World Association of World Federalists, 1954-. 4 times a year.

World Justice [Justice dans le Monde]. Louvain, Belgium: Research Center for International Social Justice, 1959-. 4 times a year.

World Politics: A Quarterly Journal of International Relations. Princeton, N.J.: Princeton University Press, 1948-.

Research in Progress

In addition to the sources listed below consult the section *Dissertation Lists* for information concerning current research.

Carnegie Endowment for International Peace. **Current Research in International Affairs.** New York: 1952, pp. 193. "This selected bibliography of work in progress by private research agencies in English-speaking countries was begun in 1948 as the December issue of the Carnegie Endowment periodical, *International Conciliation* . . . and published in that form in 1949, 1950 and 1951. Present plans are to publish it as a separate booklet less frequently than once a year. The information is based on reports regarding research programs in international relations and problems from 115 institutions. Theses, articles and speeches are not included, so that the projects listed represent major work, much of it long-term. The arrangement is by organizations, then by schools and universities, listing under each entry books, pamphlets and study projects, and individuals engaged on them. There are indexes of persons and of subjects." (Conover, p. 42)

Current Thought on Peace and War: A Semi-Annual Digest of Literature and Research in Progress on the Problems of World Order and Conflict. Durham, N.C.: 1960-. (See *Abstracts.*)

International Studies Conference. **Travaux en cours dans le domaine des relations internationales. [Works in Progress in the Field of International Relations.]** Paris: Dotation Carnegie pour la Paix Internationale, 1952, pp. 59. "A survey of research in progress in European countries, published to provide a European counterpart to the Carnegie Endowment *Current Research in International Affairs.* Data are given by country, for Austria, Germany, Belgium, Finland, France, Norway, the Netherlands, Sweden, and Switzerland. There are listed many research projects by individuals in faculties or scientific societies, and doctoral theses in press, as well as group projects. For each country the chief specialized periodicals are noted. There are separate indexes of authors and subjects, the latter all in the field of international relations." (Conover, p. 44)

Register of Research in the Social Sciences in Progress and Plan, and Directory of Research Institutions. London: Cambridge University Press, 1943-. Annual. Prepared at the National Institute of Economic and Social Research. "This 'pioneer among documentary services on current social science research,' intended primarily as a tool for research workers, was not published for sale until 1948. . . . It has been influential in stimulating other systematic records of research in progress. The coverage . . . is comprehensive for research projects of importance undertaken at universities, research institutions and other agencies in the British Isles, of which it provides in its back pages a directory and index. The lists of theses are restricted to doctoral dissertations, and an explanatory note comments that many mature scholars doing private research in the large universities have not entered their topics. There is a subject index and an index of names of research workers. . . . The explanatory notes which follow the Table of Contents are notably lucid and the guide as a whole is exceptionally easy to use." (Conover, pp. 44–45)

U.S. Department of State, Bureau of Intelligence and Research. **External Research: A List of Studies Currently in Progress.** Washington, D.C.: U.S. Government Printing Office, 1952-. This is a series of research lists for social science research carried on by private scholars throughout the United States on foreign areas listed as follows: (1) U.S.S.R. and Eastern Europe, (2) East Asia, (3) Southeast Asia, (4) South Asia, (5) Western Europe, (6) Middle East, (7) Africa, (8) American Republics, (9) British Commonwealth, (10) International Affairs. This is a revision of earlier lists, whose titles have varied. The first title was *Unpublished Research on [Subject], Completed and in Progress.* The current list includes only research in progress. Completed research is reported in separate lists published annually in the fall.

Statistics and Other Quantitative Data

Demographic Yearbook. Prepared in Collaboration with the Dept. of Social Affairs. Lake Success, N.Y.; New York, N.Y.: U.N. Statistical Office, 1949-. Annual. Demographic survey of statistics for more than 250 countries and territories on population trends, marriage, divorce, births, deaths, life expectancy.

Ginsburg, Norton Sydney. **Atlas of Economic Development.** Chicago: University of Chicago Press, 1961, pp. vii+119. Foreword by Bert F. Hoselitz. Part eight consists of a statistical analysis by Brian J. L. Berry. Includes maps, diagrams, tables, and a bibliography.

Population Index. Princeton, N.J.: Office of Population Research, Princeton University, and Population Association of America, 1935-. Quarterly. (See *Periodicals: Indexes to Periodical Articles.*)

Russett, Bruce M., *et al.* **World Handbook of Political and Social Indicators.** New Haven and London: Yale University Press, 1964, pp. x+373. A collection of statistical data regarding 133 states and colonies arranged, in Part A, for comparative purposes in a series of 75 tables, each series related to a theory of political and social change. Part B, Analysis of Trends and Patterns, analyzes the data presented. The data in this book has been reproduced on punch cards. These and code books are available from the Yale Political Data Program, or from the Inter-University Consortium for Political Research. A companion volume, **Comparing Nations: The Use of Quantitative Data in Cross-National Research,** edited by Richard L. Merritt and Stein Rokkan, is forthcoming.

Statistics Sources. Edited by Paul Wasserman, *et al.* Detroit: Gale Research Company, 1962, pp. 288. Presents both primary and secondary sources by alphabetical listing according to subject. Primarily lists American publications and organizations, with emphasis on national, rather than local or regional sources.

United Nations. **Compendium of Social Statistics.** New York: United Nations, 1963, pp. xii+586. In English and French. Prepared under the auspices of the Inter-Agency Working Party on Statistics for Social Programmes by the United Nations, the International Labour Office, the Food and Agriculture Organization of the United Nations, UNESCO, and the World Health Organization. This volume "comprises basic statistical indicators required for describing the major aspects of the social situation in the world and the regions, as well as changes and trends in the level of living" (Introduction, p. 1.) for the years 1950–1960. However, in many cases 1960 data were not available at the time of publication and the volume is expected to be revised and up-dated at some future time.

United Nations, International Labour Office. **Yearbook of Labour Statistics.** Geneva: 1936-. Annual. In French, English, and Spanish since 1941. Contains statistics concerning labor in all parts of the world, with countries listed in alphabetical order according to the English alphabet under chapters divided according to subject matter, e.g., employment, unemployment, total and economically active population, wages, etc. Appendices include tables on industrial production, exchange rates, etc.

United Nations, Statistical Office. **Monthly Bulletin of Statistics,** No. 1, August, 1946-. New York: 1947-. Monthly. In English and French. "Arrangement is by subject. . . . Provides current economic and social data for many of the tables published in the *United Nations Statistical Year-Book.*" (Walford, p. 93)

United Nations, Statistical Office. **Statistical Year Book.** New York: 1949-. Annual. "Continues the *Statistical Year-Book of the League of Nations,* 1926–1942/44 (Geneva, 1927–45). The scope has been enlarged by the United Nations to cover social and cultural statistics, in addition to the demographic and economics statistics already included. Arrangement is by subject; tables, where appropriate, are classified by the International standard industrial classification of all economic activities. Normally a twenty-year run is given for each series. Subject and country indexes. Sources are cited. Current data relating to many of the tables are published regularly in the United Nations *Monthly Bulletin of Statistics.*" (Walford, p. 93)

United Nations, Statistical Office, Department of Economic and Social Affairs. **Yearbook of International Trade Statistics.** New York: United Nations, 1949-. Data used in this yearbook are taken from official sources of the countries included, or from information supplied by the governments of these countries to the United Nations. The 1962 Yearbook shows detailed statistics for 138 countries, and summary tables showing world trade by regions and countries, world exports by provenance and destination, among others.

United Nations, Statistical Office, Department of Economic and Social Affairs. **Yearbook of National Accounts Statistics.** New York: United Nations, 1957-. In English and French. Prepared by the U.N. Statistical Office with the assistance of national statistical services. The 1964 Yearbook listed data for more than 100 countries and territories, with data for each country presented in separate chapters under uniform table headings. The presentation has been planned in such a form as to facilitate the comparison of the estimates for the various countries.

U.S. Bureau of the Census. **Statistical Abstract of the United States.** Washington, D.C.: U.S. Government Printing Office, 1878-. Annual. Designed to serve as a convenient statistical reference and as a guide to other statistical publications and sources. Each section has an introduction which gives the sources and, in the 1963 volume, a guide to State Statistical Abstracts. The editions are continually revised, new information and tables of current interest added and less timely data eliminated. Some of the subjects covered are: Population, vital statistics, immigration, law enforcement, military service, elections, banking and finance, communications, comparative international statistics, etc.

U.S. Library of Congress, Census Library Project. **Statistical Yearbooks: An Annotated Bibliography of the General Statistical Yearbooks of Major Political Subdivisions of the World.** Prepared by Phyllis G. Carter. Washington, D.C., 1953, pp. 123. (See *Bibliographies: Subject Bibliographies.*)

The World Almanac and Book of Facts. New York: New York World-Telegram, 1868-. (See *Surveys of World Events.*)

World Survey of Education: Handbook of Educational Organization and Statistics. Paris: UNESCO, 1955, pp. 943. "Detailed description and statistics of the educational systems of almost 200 countries and territories, prepared by UNESCO from the replies to a questionnaire sent to member states." (Conover, p. 56)

Surveys of World Events

Africa Diary: Weekly Diary of African Events, with Index. New Delhi: Africa Publications, 1961-. A weekly news digest covering all of Africa, individually by country as well as for the entire continent. Quarterly and annual indexes.

African Recorder: A Fortnightly Record of African Events with Index. New Delhi: 1962-. Summaries of events are entered alphabetically by country, with an added section for events relating to Africa Outside Africa. Semiannual and annual indexes.

The Annual Register of World Events. London: Longmans, Green and Co., 1759-. Title and publishers have varied. In the volume for 1963 events are surveyed according to political and geographical areas, i.e., The United Kingdom, the Commonwealth, International Organizations, The Americas, the USSR, and Eastern Europe, etc., followed by the subjects of religion, technology, biology, international law, etc.

Les Archives Internationales Pharos. Paris: Pharos, 1944-. Weekly (irregular). "French documentation service issued by the Agence Internationale de Documentation 'Pharos,' with subtitle, 'Documentation contemporaine permanente politique, économique et sociale.'" It is in three loose-leaf sections. First section is *Archives biographiques,* short biographical notes of prominent personages, French and foreign, with separate consecutive numbering for pages and biographies. Section 2 is *Archives politiques, économiques et sociales,* which "consists of factual articles or reproductions of documents, in full or in précis form; there are two or more of these fascicles, numbered consecutively as *Documents* in each issue, each treating a single significant topic of international import. . . ." Sections 1 and 2 indexed together monthly, with quarterly and annual cumulated indexes; third section is a chronology, *Archives chronologiques des événements mondiaux (Ephemérides internationales).* It has separate consecutive paging and numbering of items as well as its own monthly and cumulated index. (Conover, pp. 32–33)

Asian Recorder: A Weekly Digest of Outstanding Asian Events with Index. Delhi: Sankaran, 1955-. Weekly survey of events in all countries of Asia, arranged alphabetically, with a note as to the source. Events outside Asia listed under the heading Asia Outside Asia. Quarterly indexes with cumulative annual index.

The British Survey (Main Series). London: British Society of International Understanding, 1939-. Series of leaflets, each of which is devoted to one or more special themes. A separate leaflet provides an annual index. "Besides the Main Series, which is designed for adult orientation—'to provide the essential facts upon which people can base their own opinion about foreign and imperial affairs' is the purpose of the Society—there are published a monthly Popular Series, also on individual themes or countries and adapted to secondary schools, and a short monthly summary of world events." (Conover, p. 33)

Brookings Institution. **Major Problems of United States Foreign Policy: A Study Guide.** Washington, D.C.: 1947-. Annual. "Handbook of studies in international relations, presenting an annual survey of world affairs involving problems of foreign policy for the United States. Designed for the training of specialists, it is in form akin to investigations carried on by government policy makers, with careful factual analysis of each separate problem in the framework of an over-all view of the world situation and statement of possible alternatives of action—a technique termed the 'problem approach.' Each volume ends with a bibliographical note indicating chief general sources and a short evaluatively annotated bibliography of particularly useful documentation for study of the problems considered." (Conover, p. 48)

Chronology of International Events. 11 vols. [London]: Royal Institute of International Affairs, 1945–1955. Was published semimonthly. Together with the *World Today,* which it supplemented, superseded *Bulletin of International News.* It carries a "record of events and official documents, each described in a brief paragraph, arranged by country or international group. The cover bears a short index by subjects—agreements, conferences, disorders, speeches, reports, etc.—and an annual index is separately published, including place and personal names and chief subjects." (Conover, p. 41)

Chronology of the Second World War. London and New York: Royal

Institute of International Affairs, 1947, pp. 374. A consolidated edition of the Chronology that was published quarterly throughout the war, it eliminates the less important details, particularly those dealing with military operations, and includes some information which, during the war, was withheld for security reasons. Principal events are listed in bold type throughout the volume, and these events are alphabetized in one small section in lieu of an index which would have been unwieldy.

Facts on File: A Weekly News Digest with Cumulative Index. New York: Person's Index, Facts on File, Inc., 1940-. A weekly news digest, with cumulative indexes published twice monthly. Subjects covered include World, National, and Foreign Affairs, Economy, etc.

Foreign Policy Association. **Foreign Policy Bulletin: An Analysis of Current International Events.** New York: 1921-. Semimonthly. "An eight-page leaflet which since June 15, 1951 has replaced the former small weekly *Bulletin* and the longer fortnightly *Foreign Policy Reports,* published by the Association. Carries articles of two or more pages by specialists in international affairs, and a regular 'Spotlight' on an event or topic of particular moment, usually written by the editor, Vera Micheles Dean. Frequently facing pages present articles by two writers on opposing sides of a controversial issue. The purpose of the Association is to carry on research and educational activities to aid in the understanding and constructive development of American foreign policy, and the *Bulletin* is addressed primarily to study groups, the articles written in clear explanatory style, with adequate background detail." (Conover, p. 36)

Keesing's Contemporary Archives: Weekly Diary of World Events with Index Continually Kept Up-to-Date. London: Keesing's Ltd., 1931-. A weekly survey of reports, statistics, and data summarized and translated from British and foreign news sources, and international organizations. Subject indexes, cumulative fortnightly, quarterly, annually, triennually.

The New International Year Book: A Compendium of the World's Progress for the Year. New York: Funk and Wagnalls, 1932-. Contains a chronology of world events for each day of the year, preceding the yearbook. Illustrations, maps, charts, and diagrams are separately indexed. The form is that of an encyclopedia, with information on each subject related to the events of the year.

News from Behind the Iron Curtain. New York: Free Europe Press, Free Europe Committee, 1952-. Monthly. "Informational journal for which much of the material is selected from that used in the program Radio Free Europe of the Free Europe Committee (which until April 1954 was known as the National Committee for a Free Europe), or gathered from the work of the Committee's Mid-European Studies Center. The magazine has fifty-odd pages in each issue, with some photographs. It carries lead articles on politics, economics, culture, and other aspects of the Soviet-dominated countries, a review of the month's events, and news notes on current developments. Sources used are largely the press and documents of the countries studied and testimony of recent refugees." (Conover, p. 82)

The New York Times Index. New York: New York Times, 1913-. (See *Newspapers: Indexes to Articles.*)

Revue Politique et Parlementaire. Paris: 1894-.

Royal Institute of International Affairs. **Survey of International Affairs.** London: Oxford University Press, 1925-. 3 supplements. Formerly edited by Arnold Toynbee. Deals with world affairs in a series of papers on various problems. Published annually, with some exceptions when a period of more than one year is covered in a single volume. The 1956–1958 volume was a result of contributions from nine writers on the staff of the Royal Institute for World Affairs, with G. Barraclough as editor, and covered the Suez Crisis, and those in Poland and Hungary, also giving extensive consideration to the emerging nations, underdeveloped areas, East-West relations, etc.

Swiss Review of World Affairs. Zurich: 1951-. A publication of the *Neue Zürcher Zeitung.* "Magazine of about 30 pages put out by a Swiss daily which is considered one of the best newspapers of Europe. The articles and editorials present informed comment on conditions and events in the international scene." (Conover, p. 39)

United Nations, Dept. of Economic Affairs. **World Economic Report.** New York: 1945/47-. Annual. "Comprehensive review of world economic conditions, designed primarily for the use of the Economic and Social Council and other organs of U.N. in formulating recommendations in the economic field. The analysis is in two parts, the first reviewing major changes in domestic economy of groups of nations, the second surveying international trade and payments.

. . . The text is in essay style, interspersed with statistical tables. There is a full index of subjects, with itemization under names of countries." (Conover, p. 58)

The United States in World Affairs. New York and London: Published for the Council on Foreign Relations by Harper & Bros., 1932-. Annual. "Succinct review of world conditions, tensions, and problems in their relation to American foreign affairs, begun almost a quarter century ago under the editorship of Walter Lippmann. . . . Detailed information on the various phases and areas of foreign interests of the United States is presented in a running text of dispassionate and factual analysis. The text is documented with footnote references, and concluded with a Selected Bibliography that contains much documentary and periodical material, a Chronology of World Events for the year, and a subject index." (Conover, p. 54)

The World Almanac and Book of Facts. New York World Telegram and Sun: 1868-. Published annually except between the years 1876 and 1886. It is designed to be a comprehensive record of American and foreign activities, with information concerning current politics in the U.S.; summary of world events; tables of election returns, both national and state, in election years; lists of government officials and members of Congress; a chronology of world events, under national, foreign, U.N. and general categories, by month; and a variety of other facts.

The World Today. Chatham House Review. London: Royal Institute of International Affairs, 1945-. Monthly. "This small journal of the Royal Institute, which supersedes an earlier *Bulletin of International News,* carries objective reports on the international scene. The first few pages are Notes of the Month, short factual statements of specially significant immediate occurrences. Then come interpretative articles on current conditions in individual countries, with sufficient background for orientation; these are usually contributed by correspondents on the spot, who sign with initials. Over a two-year period, coverage is given to almost all major nations. There is an annual index of subjects." (Conover, pp. 40–41)

Year Book of World Affairs. Published under the auspices of the London Institute of World Affairs. London: Stevens and Sons, 1947-. The annual volume for 1964 consists of two major parts. The first is a series of articles by scholars from various countries on world affairs including such titles as The United States and the

British Deterrent, The Alliance for Progress, Indonesia and the Malaysia Issue, and Recent Developments in the Theory of International Relations. The second part consists of reviews of books published during the year on subjects relevant to world problems and events. There is an index to the books reviewed, which in the 1964 edition numbered approximately 400.

Treaty Collections

Great Britain, Foreign Office. **British and Foreign State Papers.** London: H.M. Stationery Office, 1841-. Formerly printed exclusively for the use of the Government and its diplomatic agents, but later published because of their general interest. First published by Ridgway and Sons, London. These publications contain the principal documents which have been made public, relating to political and commercial affairs and relations between nations. Documents in Vol. 1 are arranged chronologically. Systematic collection began in 1813. There is an index for each volume, alphabetical by country and subject in earlier volumes; later volumes include both a chronological and an alphabetical index. Beginning with Vol. 116, *Hertslet's Commercial Treaties* were incorporated into the *Foreign and State Papers.* Vol. 161, published in 1963, contained papers for 1954; several volumes have been issued periodically as indexes, and these cover most of the series. Indexes are Vols. 64, 93, 115, 138.

League of Nations. **Treaty Series: Publication of Treaties and International Engagements Registered with the Secretariat of the League.** Vols. 1–205. (Treaty No. 1-4834) Sept. 1920–1944/46. London: Harrison, 1920–1946. General index, 1920–1946. Nos. 1–9 (for vols. 1–205). Geneva: 1927–1946. 9 vols. Includes treaties between the members and also between members and nonmembers. Translations in French and English.

Slusser, Robert M., and Triska, Jan F. **A Calendar of Soviet Treaties, 1917–1957.** With the assistance of George Ginsburgs and Wilfred O. Reiners. Stanford, California: Stanford University Press, 1959, pp. xii+530. This volume is No. 4 in the Hoover Institution on War, Revolution, and Peace Documentary Series. The purpose of the volume, according to the authors, was to identify as fully and accurately as possible the treaties and other international agreements concluded by Soviet Russia from 1917 through the end of 1957. The volume, complete in itself, is the first of two volumes. The second, by the same authors, is *The Theory, Law, and Policy of Soviet Treaties.*

114

Triska, Jan F., and Slusser, Robert M. **The Theory, Law, and Policy of Soviet Treaties.** Stanford, California: Stanford University Press, 1962, pp. xi+593. This is the second volume in a study of Soviet contractual arrangements with other states. The first volume was *A Calendar of Soviet Treaties, 1917–1957,* by the same authors. The present volume "is essentially an attempt to extract and analyze the salient features and the more enduring tendencies, conditions, and trends which help to explain the making of Soviet treaty theory, law, and policy; to identify their common denominators; and to apply the resulting pattern to an over-all long-term analysis of Soviet international agreements." (Introduction)

United Nations. **Treaty Series: Treaties and International Agreements Registered or Filed and Recorded with the Secretariat of the United Nations.** New York: United Nations, 1946-. Beginning December 14, 1946, publishes the text of every treaty and international agreement entered into by any member of the United Nations. These must be registered with the Secretariat and published according to Article 102 of the United Nations Charter. Text is in English and French. All treaties in a volume are listed in a table of contents chronologically in the order of registration.

United Nations, Office of Legal Affairs. **List of Treaty Collections.** New York: 1956, pp. 174. Compiled by the Codification Division of the U.N. Office of Legal Affairs, the list is "limited, in principle, to collections published in and after the last two decades of the 18th century." (Introduction) Part I is devoted to General Collections and also includes indexes, chronologies, bibliographies relating to treaties in general and handbooks. Part II lists collections by subject matter, and Part III lists collections by country. The lists are chronological according to the periods covered by the collections. Mostly in English, some French. Indexed.

U.S. Department of State. **Catalogue of Treaties, 1814–1918.** Washington, D.C.: U.S. Government Printing Office, 1919, pp. 716+xxv. Originally begun as a card catalog, it does not claim to be complete, either in regard to treaties listed or to text references. The period after 1900 has been emphasized. Treaties are arranged in chronological lists, giving time and place of signature and ratification, signatory powers, collections in which the text can be found, with cross-references to later treaties which abrogate or modify the treaty in question. The index is in two parts: One is an index by country; two is an index of agreements of a general international nature. There is also an appendix listing selected treaties from 1353 to 1814.

U.S. Department of State. **List of Treaties Submitted to the Senate, 1789–1934.** Washington, D.C.: U.S. Government Printing Office, 1935, pp. 138. A list of all treaties (the term includes international agreements of all forms) submitted to the Senate from the beginning of the 1st Congress to the close of the 73rd Congress, inclusive, with the exception of treaties with Indian tribes. Treaties are listed in chronological order by date of signature. Also given for each treaty are names of the other party (given as "multilateral" if there are several parties), the first date of submission to the Senate, other dates if the treaty has been resubmitted one or more times, the Treaty Series number for those treaties which are in force, and the action, if any, taken on the submitted treaty. In addition to the chronological and tabular list of treaties submitted, there is a section giving notes on many of the treaties.

Also published by the State Department are:

U.S. Department of State. **Treaties Submitted to the Senate, 1935–1939.** Washington, D.C.: U.S. Government Printing Office, 1940, pp. 20.

U.S. Department of State. **Treaties Submitted to the Senate, 1935–1944.** Washington, D.C.: U.S. Government Printing Office, 1945, pp. iii+28.

These give procedure on treaties and their status as of the dates given in the title.

U.S. Department of State. **United States Treaties and Other International Agreements.** Washington, D.C.: U.S. Government Printing Office, 1952-. This series is the official publication of all agreements and treaties to which the United States becomes a party. Agreements and treaties from 1950 onward are printed in this form, those for 1950 having been printed in 1952. Prior to the publication of this compilation, treaties and other international agreements were officially printed in the *U.S. Statutes at Large.* This present series constitutes the legal evidence for the treaties contained therein as did the *U.S. Statutes at Large* for the treaties and agreements which were published there.

Each volume lists all the documents it contains on its first pages. There is a complete record of each agreement, treaty, convention, etc. from its inception until it is entered into force. Correspondence, conferences, etc. are given in the languages used by the parties, signatories, etc. The documents are arranged according to date from earliest in the year to latest. There may be more than one volume per year. The agreements are arranged here in the numerical order in which they are published by the State Department in pamphlet form in the *Treaties and Other International Acts Series.* Any missing numbers are those agreements that had entered into force prior to 1950 and thus appear in the *Statutes at Large.*

U.S. Department of State. **Treaties and Other International Acts Series.** Washington, D.C.: U.S. Government Printing Office, 1946-. This pamphlet Series, already referred to, makes available in a single series the texts of treaties and other instruments (constitutions, charters of international organizations, declarations, agreements, etc.) which establish or define relations between the United States and other countries. This series combines two former series published by the State Department, *Executive Agreement Series* and *Treaty Series.* These are published in pamphlet form and begin with No. 1501. They are listed in the *Monthly Catalog* under State Department publications.

U.S. Department of State, Office of the Legal Advisor. **Treaties in Force: A List of Treaties and Other International Agreements of the United States.** Washington, D.C.: U.S. Department of State, 1929-. Annual. Title has varied. Includes list of all treaties and other international agreements to which the U.S. is a party, and which are in force as of the title date (January 1,——). The list is in two parts, with an appendix. The first part contains bilateral treaties and agreements, listed by country, with subject headings. The second part includes multilateral treaties and agreements, listed by subject heading. *A List of Treaties and Other International Acts of the United States of America in Force* was the former title.

U.S. Treaties. **Treaties, Conventions, International Acts, Protocols and Agreements Between the United States of America and Other Powers, 1776–1937.** 4 vols. Washington, D.C.: U.S. Government Printing Office, 1910–1938. These volumes were compiled pursuant to various resolutions of the U.S. Senate from January 18, 1909 to May 24, 1937, under the direction of the Senate Committee on Foreign Relations. The first two volumes were compiled by William Malloy. The first two volumes contain a chronological list of all treaties from 1778 to 1909. These volumes then list the treaties alphabetically, including the particulars. Vol. II contains a section dealing with International Conventions and Acts. Vol. III was compiled in 1923 and Vol. IV in 1938. Treaties in the fourth volume date from October 1, 1929 to December 31, 1937. The volumes vary slightly from one another in arrangement. These volumes have been printed as Senate Documents and can be found also in the *Congressional Serial Set.*

U.S. Treaties. **Treaties and Other International Acts of the United States of America.** 8 vols. Edited by Hunter Miller. Washington, D.C.: U.S. Government Printing Office, 1931–1948. These volumes include all the international acts of the United States that have ever been in effect for the period covered by the volumes (1776– 1863). The original plan by Dr. Hunter Miller, the editor, was to cover the period from 1776 through December 31, 1930. However, this was not accomplished before his retirement, and the last publication in the series was Vol. VIII published in 1948. The original plan included the publication of a global index after the series was completed and for Vol. I to be printed in its final form after all the document volumes to which it refers had been published. The present form is incomplete and provisional. However it does include, since the earliest papers were prior to the Constitution, a table of Presidents of the Continental Congress and a note regarding two Secretaries for Foreign Affairs from 1781 through 1789. Vols. II through VIII are the document volumes, and in these, documents are arranged chronologically according to the date of the signature. The documents carry serial numbers in the volumes, but these are simply for convenience and have no significance aside from that. All international acts of the United States which have gone into force in the period covered are included, whether they are now in force or not. Each volume also includes related papers, and notes follow each document, which give some of the diplomatic history of the document. There are cross-references to numbers of the *Treaty Series* and the *Executive Agreement Series,* generally before each document printed—the lack of such numbers means that the document in question is not in either series. (See *Treaties and Other International Acts Series,* p. 117.)

Yearbooks

General

Europa Yearbook. London: Europa Publications, 1926-. Formerly titled *Europa*. Since 1960 has been issued in two volumes. Volume I, Part I deals with international organizations; the 1964 edition introduced a comprehensive index to these organizations. Part II of Vol. I is devoted to the countries of Europe, with information on governments, political parties, judicial systems, etc. included. Vol. II deals with Africa, the Americas, Asia, Australasia in the same manner. There is a listing of diplomatic personnel for each country.

European Year Book. The Hague: Nijhoff; London: Batsford, 1955-. (See *International Organizations: Other*.)

International Court of Justice. **Yearbook.** The Netherlands: Registry of the International Court of Justice, 1947-. (See *International Court of Justice*, Series D, in the section *International Law*.)

International Yearbook of Political Behavior Research. Glencoe, Illinois: Free Press of Glencoe, 1961-. General purpose of the yearbook is to facilitate the publication of venturesome efforts at the frontiers of political science and other behavioral sciences. Under the direction of a special editor, each volume concentrates on one significant area of political inquiry (e.g., the Community Political System, Military Politics, Judicial Decision-Making), the various contributors covering relevant empirical research, scientific method, or political theory.

The International Yearbook and Statesmen's Who's Who. London: Burke's Peerage, 1953-. " 'The purpose of the volume is to give information on the economic and political structure of each country in the world, followed by the biographies of the principal persons in each country.' International organizations; reigning royal families; and charts showing the organization of the foreign ministries of the U.K., U.S.A., France, U.S.S.R., and China. The information on individual countries is similar to that in the *States-*

119

men's Year Book (but without the bibliographies). The Who's Who
has 10,000 biographies, similar to those in the *International Who's
Who* (which has 18,000). Entries are based on questionnaires and
the draft is submitted to the biographee before publication." (Walford, p. 94)

League of Nations Secretariat, Information Section. **The League from
Year to Year.** Geneva: Information Section, League of Nations,
1927/28–1938. (See *International Organizations: League of Nations.*)

**Orbis, the Encyclopaedia of Extra-European Countries: A Survey
and Directory of Political, Industrial, Financial, Cultural and
Scientific Organizations in the Continents of Africa, America, Asia
and Australasia, Arranged Alphabetically under Countries.** London: Europa Publications, 1950-. Loose-leaf. 6 supplements a year.
Supersedes earlier editions. An international manual which brings
selective directories of business, industry, press, etc., together with
political and statistical data for all countries. Each binder is com-
posed of a collection of separately numbered sets of pages for
individual countries.

Ottlik, Georges, ed. **Annuaire de la Société des Nations.** 8 vols.
Geneva: Payot et cie., 1927–1938. (See *International Organizations:
League of Nations.*)

Political Handbook of the World: Parliaments, Parties and Press.
New York: For Council on Foreign Relations, Inc., by Harper and
Row [c. 1927]-. An annual publication "designed to furnish the
necessary factual background for understanding political events in
all countries which have independent governments . . ." For each
country there is information given as to capital, area (in square
miles), population, the chief of state, governing body, parliament or
national assembly, cabinet, political parties, their leaders, recent political events, and the national press.

**Statesman's Year Book: Statistical and Historical Annual of the States
of the World.** London and New York: Macmillan, 1864-. Illustrations, maps. Annual. Gives descriptions and statistical information
concerning International Organizations (United Nations and others);
the Commonwealth countries; the United States of America (including data on each of the states); and the remaining countries of
the world. For example the 1964 edition gives the following information about each country: its history or the description of its
government or both; in some cases the constitution is described,

as is the area and population, vital statistics, religion, education, health and social welfare, justice, finance, defense, production, communications, currency and banking. Reference works are also listed for most of the countries. Of interest to the student of International Relations is the fact that diplomatic representatives and their addresses are also listed for each country.

Union of International Associations. **Yearbook of International Organizations.** Brussels: U.I.A., 1948-. (See *International Organizations: Others.*)

United Nations. **Yearbook of the United Nations.** Lake Success, N.Y.; New York, N.Y.: United Nations Department of Public Information, 1947-. (See *International Organizations: United Nations, Activities and General Information.*)

United Nations, International Labour Office. **Yearbook of Labour Statistics.** Geneva: 1936-. (See *Statistics.*)

National

The Arab Directory for Commerce, Industry, and Liberal Professions in the Arab Countries. Anglo-Arab-French Edition. Beirut, Lebanon: 1945-. Annual. Text in English, Arabic, and French. Includes index to headings and to advertisers, plus a general information and commercial directory for the Arabic countries, a section which summarizes the geographical situation of each country, population, economic resources, trade, industry, and communications, as well as listing specific companies by city, according to type of commerce or industry.

Australia, Commonwealth Bureau of Census and Statistics. **Official Yearbook of the Commonwealth of Australia.** Canberra: Government Printing Office, 1908-. Annual. "Supplemented by the *Quarterly Summary of Australian Statistics.* Largely a statistical work, but has historical and other material including a chronological table of events since 1788. Includes the *Select List of Books About, or Published in, Australia,* compiled by the National Library, and also available separately. Index of special articles included in previous issues. The individual states also issue yearbooks." (Walford, p. 102)

The British Yearbook of International Law. London: Oxford University Press, 1920-. (See *International Law.*)

Canada, Bureau of Statistics. **Canada Yearbook: The Official Statistical Annual of the Resources, History, Institutions, and Social and Economic Conditions of the Dominion.** Ottawa, 1906-. Maps. Annual.

China Yearbook. Shanghai: North China Daily News and Herald, Ltd., 1931–1939. Published 1912 to 1919, London: Routledge; New York: Dutton. From 1921 to 1929 published in Tientsin by the Tientsin Press. Publication was disrupted by the Sino-Japanese War, which in the final volume was dealt with "entirely on the basis of official documents or speeches." The last volume included in addition to those, new sections on the Currency Problem during the hostilities, the establishment and operations of the Federal Reserve Bank, Japan's Programme for Economic Development in China, the Japanese-sponsored Customs Tariffs, and the Flora of China. There are two appendixes, the second dealing with a Review of Chinese War Finance. Also included are a Who's Who, and a chapter on The Kuomintang and the Government.

Great Britain, Central Office of Information. **Britain: An Official Handbook.** London: H.M. Stationery Office, 1946-. Annual, from 1954. Illustrated. Maps. "Excellent summaries of institutions and life in Britain. Sections (1956 ed.): The British Isles.—Government and administration.—Defence.—The national economy.—Industry.—Transport and communications.—Labour.—Finance.—Trade.—Social welfare.—Housing and planning.—Religion, science and the arts.—Sound and television broadcasting.—The press. The tables provide the latest available statistics. Detailed index. A model of what such an official handbook should be." (Walford, p. 95)

Handbook on People's China. Peking: Foreign Languages Press, 1957, pp. 236. "Gives detailed facts and figures, plus more general background information on Communist China, its social and economic development, especially since 1949." (Walford, p. 99)

India: A Reference Annual. Delhi: Ministry of Information, 1953-. Map. Annual. "Includes chronology of events from 3000 B.C.; bibliographies are appended to each chapter." (Walford, p. 100)

Israel, Central Office of Information. **Government Yearbook.** Tel

Aviv: Government Printer, 1950-. Annual. "Gives comprehensive data, including texts of principal legislation passed in the previous year. The statistical section is also published separately as *Statistical Abstract of Israel,* 1951-, covering 1949/50-. The Hebrew edition includes a bibliography of books published in the previous year (e.g., the *Yearbook* issued in 1955 lists books which appeared between April 1954 and March 1955)." (Walford, p. 100)

The Israel Yearbook. Tel Aviv: Israel Publications, 1946-. Annual. Previously published as *Anglo-Palestine Yearbook,* 1946–1950. Includes a brief trades directory.

The Japan Yearbook. Tokyo: 1906-. Gives information concerning the Imperial Court, geography and population of Japan, outline of its cultural history, the government, parties and politics, public finance, commerce and industry, foreign trade, religion, literature, etc. From 1946/1948 on, published by The Foreign Affairs Association of Japan. Not published from 1931 to 1946.

The Middle East. London: Europa Publications, 1948-. The subtitle of the 1963 edition is "A survey and directory of Aden (South Arabia), Cyprus, Iran, Iraq, Israel, Jordan, Kuwait, Lebanon, Libya, Muscat and Oman, The Persian Gulf Principalities, Saudi Arabia, The Sudan, The Syrian Arab Republic, Turkey, The United Arab Republic (Egypt) and The Yemen, with geographical, historical, and economic surveys, concise information about political, industrial, financial, cultural and educational organizations, and Who's Who in the Middle East." Part I of the 1963 volume is a General Survey, including such topics as The Tenets of Islam, United Nations in the Middle East, Oil in the Middle East, and Plan for a Federal United Arab Republic. Part II deals with each territory separately.

Pakistan, 1955–56. Karachi: Pakistan Publications, [1956], pp. 364. "Law and administration, economics, public services, defence, welfare, foreign affairs; brief sections on East and West Pakistan, Karachi and Kashmir." (Walford, p. 100)

The South American Handbook: A Yearbook and Guide to the Countries and Resources of South and Central America, Mexico and Cuba. London: Trade and Travel, 1924-. Maps. Annual. "Initially published as the *Anglo-South American Handbook, 1921–22.* Gives detailed information on each of the 23 countries concerned, covering physical features, climate, principal products, industry, natural resources, government, foreign trade, transport, currency, and weights and measures. Leading cities are described separately and hints are provided for commercial travellers. 8 coloured maps." (Walford, p. 102)

The Times of India Directory and Yearbook, including Who's Who. Bombay and London: Bennett, Coleman, 1915-. Maps. Annual. Listed separately under the names of each state and territory is political information such as the names of members of the cabinet, ministers, political parties, etc. Also listed are commercial firms, trades, and professions within each. General information is included also and such items are listed as the composition of various political parties, their positions on various matters, their officials, etc.; Public Health; The Official Language Problem; U.S. Aid to India; Refugees and Rehabilitation; Scheduled Castes, Scheduled Tribes, and Backward Classes.

Index

Abbreviations: Abs. = Abstract(s); Assn. = Association(s); Bibl. = Bibliography, Bibliographies, *or* Bibliographie; Biog. = Biography *or* Biographies; Cat. = Catalog(s) *or* Catalogue(s); Enc. = Encyclopedia(s) *or* Encyclopaedia(s); Inst. = Institution(s) *or* Institute(s); Intern. = International, Internationale(s), *or* Internationaux; Jour. = Journal(s); Lit. = Literature *or* Literatur; Pub. = Publication(s); Supp. = Supplement(s); Vol. = Volume(s).